3/08/91

To Bobbie, My good friend who could have written this book.
Read, Understand Yourself and be as gentle and loving with Bobbie as you are with others.

Love,
Elizabeth

ONE PERSON CAN
MAKE A
DIFFERENCE

BOOKS BY THE SAME AUTHOR

Out of Darkness Into the Light

To Give Is To Receive:
An 18 Day
Course On Healing Relationships

Love Is Letting Go Of Fear

Teach Only Love

Goodbye To Guilt

Love Is The Answer

AND ON BANTAM AUDIO CASSETTES:

To Give is To Receive

Teach Only Love

Introduction to a Course in Miracles

Forgiveness is the Key to Happiness

For information on Jerry Jampolsky's lecture and
workshop schedule as well as information on audio and video cassette tapes, please send a self
addressed envelope to:

Gerald G. Jampolsky, M.D.
c/o Mini Course
P.O. Box 1012
Tiburon, CA 94920

ONE PERSON CAN MAKE A DIFFERENCE

Ordinary People Doing Extraordinary Things

Gerald G. Jampolsky, M.D.

BANTAM BOOKS

NEW YORK • TORONTO • LONDON • SYDNEY • AUCKLAND

ONE PERSON CAN MAKE A DIFFERENCE
A Bantam Book / December 1990

Library of Congress Cataloging-in-Publication Data
Jampolsky, Gerald G., 1925-
    One person can make a difference: ordinary people doing
extraordinary things/Gerald Jampolsky.
        p.   cm.
    ISBN 0-553-07025-8
    1. Biography—20th century.   2. Love.   3. Creative ability.
I. Title.
CT120.J36   1990
920'.009'04—dc20
[B]   90-796
                                                        CIP

Published simultaneously in the United States and Canada

Bantam Books are published by Bantam Books, a division of Bantam
Doubleday Dell Publishing Group, Inc. Its trademark, consisting of the
words "Bantam Books" and the portrayal of a rooster, is Registered in
U.S. Patent and Trademark Office and in other countries. Marca
Registrada. Bantam Books, 666 Fifth Avenue, New York, New York 10103.

PRINTED IN THE UNITED STATES OF AMERICA
RRH   0 9 8 7 6 5 4 3 2 1

This book is dedicated
to the innocent child
who is always alive within each of us—
who sees no obstacles,
no problems or negativity;
who doesn't believe in words
like *can't* and *impossible*,
who is not blocked
by hurtful experiences of the past,
who trusts and has faith in love,
who always knows that our purpose
is to give love to others,
to accept love for ourselves,
and to know that happiness and joy
are truly our natural state of being.

ACKNOWLEDGMENTS

I wish to express my heartfelt thanks to Hal Zina Bennett for his friendship and loving support in assisting me with the editing of this book and helping to make it a joyful process. I am also most grateful to Michelle Rapkin, senior editor at Bantam Books, for her continued support and encouragement.

The quotations that appear before each chapter are from *A Course in Miracles,* published by the Foundation for Inner Peace (P.O. Box 635, Tiburon, CA 94920), and are reprinted here with the permission of the publisher. I'd like to express my continued gratefulness to Judy Skutch Whitson and Bob Skutch for their permission to quote from this material.

CONTENTS

When you believe in something,
you have made it true.

In my travels there are more and more people coming up to me to say, "I want to be helpful and to find some place where I can volunteer and make a contribution. But I just don't know how or where to begin." My most frequent answer is, "Right from the start, follow your heart."

I find that this answer holds true even though we are living in a world where the messages we receive from others are often: "Don't follow your heart or you'll get hurt," or, "It's dangerous to stick your neck out for other people," or, "It's a fearful world that we live in; take care of yourself and your own family and let others take care of themselves."

In spite of these messages, more and more people are hearing an "inner calling," a voice from within stating that the way to make a difference in the world is to be helpful to others. It is as if the very soul of humankind is crying out to be expressed in this way, to be made fully alive through giving to others.

This is a book about people who listened to their hearts with all their might and who have truly made a significant difference. Some are people whose names are known all over the world, while others are known only to their own circle of friends. But we learn from their stories that they are all ordinary people who have done extraordinary things. In one sense, this can be looked upon as a "how to" book in which these people are our exceptional teachers, offering us guidance for one of the most simple and yet profound lessons any of us can learn: "To give is to receive."

One of the common denominators I found in these people is that they learned to believe in themselves, to turn deaf ears to those who said there were limitations or who claimed that some things simply couldn't be done. All these wonderful people, some young, some old, did not believe in words such as *can't* or *impossible.* They each chose not to accept or believe in limitation of any kind. They learned to believe in themselves and to follow the fire of compassion and love that was burning in the very center of their beings, inspiring them to follow their hearts.

The people in this book faced many obstacles, but rather than concentrating on those obstacles they focused on the solutions. Their power came from trusting and having faith in love. They remind me of that one flower on the mountain that finds a place to grow and blossom even though it appears that everything is solid rock and there is no place to grow. These people knew that with faith in love—even though that faith seemed no larger than a mustard seed—nothing was impossible. What others might have perceived as obstacles dissolved, revealing that we all have, in even that mustard seed of faith, the power to share and extend our love to others.

In talking with these people and getting to know them, I felt that each one innately knew that his own healing was somehow related to his desire and willingness to help others. None of them were people who "sort of" did things, or who merely "tried." These people made it their top priority to help others; their great tenacity simply would not allow any obstacles to stand in the way of achieving their goals. As you will see, all of them gave one hundred percent of themselves and more. They were clear that their central motivation was to give, not to get, and that in everything they did their purpose was to teach only love, not fear.

My motivation for writing this book goes back to my childhood. When I was a youngster, I had a teacher who often read books to us, and I found that my favorites were biographies. I loved hearing about real people who overcame great difficulties and succeeded in making a difference in the world. Similarly, my parents, by the example of their lives, taught that if you focused all of your energy, and if you worked hard enough and long enough, you could achieve any goal. For my two brothers and me that lesson was deeply ingrained, as permanent and indelible as tattoos on our skin.

Of all the many things my parents taught me, what always stands out most prominently in my mind is the belief that each of us can make a difference. We can each choose to live a life in which we can say, when we die, that the world is a better place for our having been here.

My parents were always much better at giving than at receiving. During holidays such as Christmas, they always gave gifts to the mailman, the ice man, the garbage man, and the paperboy. They received great pleasure from giving in this way.

My parents, who were immigrants, were very proud of the fact that they had accomplished the seemingly impossible by coming to a new country and establishing themselves in a new community. They had come from the old country, from lives that had been very difficult, and they had succeeded in establishing their own business of selling dried dates and figs.

They chose to live not so much for themselves as for

their children. They wanted to make certain that we, their three sons, had good educations so that we might accomplish things that had been beyond their own reach. Through much hard work and personal sacrifice, they accomplished what they'd set out to do, and more. My dad was particularly proud because he had achieved his goals without any formal education.

Through my parents I learned to look upon life as a challenge, and I think that this is one of the reasons why I like biographies so much. Reading was difficult for me, because I was dyslexic, but I loved reading about people who faced incredible challenges in life and conquered them. For me, these true adventures were much more exciting and interesting than fiction or fantasy.

The people I read about became role models for me. In both my childhood and early adulthood, I was plagued by negative, self-defeating, self-deprecating thoughts and feelings. As I read about people who had overcome difficult challenges, there always seemed to be a glimmering light from within that maybe someday I too could contribute something meaningful to the world. Even then, with all my self-doubts and fears, there was a part of me that believed that it might be possible to live in this world without limiting myself, and to believe that nothing is impossible.

Today it is my earnest belief that we can always find positive role models to identify with in our lives. We may find these role models in people we have actually met or will meet; we may find them in people we have only read about; or we may find them in people who have died but whose lives continue to inspire us all.

The purpose of this book is to inspire and remind both you, the reader, and me that each of us can make a difference. It is a book for all ages, because I firmly believe that whether one is three months old, three years old, or even a hundred and three, each of us can make a difference. Neither youth nor old age need ever be a barrier. I hope the stories in this book will serve as living seeds of inspired, creative thought and action for all of us, regardless of age or social or economic standing.

Perhaps the biggest limitation we can ever put on ourselves is to believe in fear rather than love. At those times in our lives when we are feeling frustration, futility, and hopelessness, we are tempted to believe that we are victims and that we must continue to suffer. Sometimes it truly seems that there is nothing we can do to get out of our situation. In a similar way, many of us have had such horrendously painful experiences that we have adopted the belief that the past will repeat itself. We let fear and anger invade our hearts, and we live as if our only goal is to survive rather than to live. It is so difficult at those times to believe the lessons taught by the teachers presented in this book, that to give is to receive.

This book is about people who are making a difference and who continue to inspire me to be more than I ever thought I could be. I hope that their stories and the lessons they have to teach will inspire you too. My fondest hope is that they will not just inspire you but will create in you an irresistible energy, putting wings on your heart that will allow you to fly beyond all self-imposed limitations.

I believe these stories will allow us all to take a fresh look at ourselves and at our purpose in life, so that we can recognize and honor our uniqueness, our humanness, and the essence of love that we truly are as individuals. Each of these stories, in its own way, tells about love and compassion for our planet, for all of humankind, and for all that is living in the universe.

As we all know, only too well, human beings can be most complex. As we look at one another, perception can be very deceptive and misleading. It can lead us to judge others as good or bad, innocent or guilty. There are many different windows through which we can choose to look at one another. I have chosen to look at the people in this book through the window of love.

All too often, the personality-self, our ego, deceives us. It tells us that what is important in this world is how much we do or how much we accomplish. However, nearly every day I am reminded of the words of Mother Teresa, who, at a time in my life when I was depressed and feeling that I was not accomplishing enough, told me that what was important in life was not how much we do or accomplish but how much love we give. She went on to say that it is our intentions that are most important and that we experience the peace of God when our thoughts and actions come from the heart of love.

Over and over again, my experiences lead me to believe that when we look at one another through the heart, a whole new reality unfolds. As we begin to reexperience ourselves as love and give that love to others in whatever creative ways our hearts tell us to, we begin to have a spiritual transformation. And by that very process the world we perceive begins to change; what had been a world filled with fear and hopelessness begins transforming into a world of love and hope.

Gifts of love can never be measured. When we are giving love there are no small or large gifts. All gifts of love are the same—boundless, complete, and nonexclusive, always extending out toward others, and always expanding without limitations.

Perhaps our number-one challenge is to let go of all of our fear and guilt and to ask for guidance from our

Higher Selves each moment of each day. As we learn to listen to the answers from within, we discover how we can direct our minds, in the most creative ways, to have only loving thoughts, words, and actions, bringing more joining, love, and joy into the world.

Each of us can make a difference when we see that our purpose in being here is to give the gift of unconditional love to all others in our lives, and to forgive.

May your reading this book encourage you to love, nourish, and cherish this innocent child within all of us, dedicating each moment of the day to it.

1

ZALINDA DORCHEOUS

Forgiveness is the key to happiness.

Although there have been numerous articles and books about forgiveness, forgiveness still is not an easy concept for most of us to internalize and apply in practical ways. Perhaps one of the difficulties is that we rarely meet people in our own lives who demonstrate total forgiveness.

One of the ways that we learn concepts such as forgiveness is through role models—that is, people who exemplify the process or principle that we would like to incorporate into our own lives. I would like to share with you a story about a woman who has become a cherished friend as well as a most important teacher for me on what forgiveness is all about.

In early 1988, I received a letter from a woman named Zalinda Dorcheous. Her message and her story turned out to be both unusual and important, helping not only me but many others who heard it. Let me tell you about that letter, written on December 26, 1987.

Zalinda began by saying that she had written to me many, many times in the past but had never mailed her letters. This time, she said, she felt a real need not only to finish the letter but to mail it.

She then told the following story: "In August of 1979, my second son, John, who was twenty years old, was murdered. I could write a book telling how his murder has changed my life and the lives of my family and friends.

"The man who killed John was tried, convicted, and sent to prison on second-degree-murder charges. After a few years he started the process of trying to get out of prison. When I heard of this I fought him through the system, a battle that went on for many years. During this battle I felt anger and pain that I had never experienced before and which I find difficult to explain even to this day.

"Then I began attending an Attitudinal Healing group in Boise, Idaho, and I was learning to look at things differently. During this time I also became a student of *A Course in Miracles*. For reasons that I did not at first understand, I started meeting with the man who was in prison for killing my son. We met once a week and I worked very hard on forgiveness. I was surprised to discover that forgiveness turned out to be not very hard at all."

The following words jumped out at me as I read her letter: "I have grown not only to like him but I want to help him." She admitted that there were many issues she needed to work on and suspected it would probably be an ongoing process. "Sometimes," she said, "I do not understand myself what is happening. I only know I am doing what I have to do and it feels good. I have had enough of the pain and anger."

She went on to say how fortunate she felt that the man who had murdered her son was willing to go through this process with her, with the help of a "really terrific and caring" psychologist. She added, "I have shared your books *Teach Only Love, Love Is Letting Go of Fear*, and *Goodbye to Guilt* with both of them."

In her letter Zalinda told me that she wanted to know what I thought about having Attitudinal Healing groups in prisons. She felt this was something that might be an important part of her life path.

She closed her letter to me with the following: "Most of all I need to thank you for the beautiful influence and help your teaching has been to me. More and more I can feel myself coming from the heart with peace and love. It feels really good and I love it! Now I want to give it back. Thank you."

Zalinda's letter taught me that I never really know in advance what a significant role any particular letter might play in my life; also, that I never know when or where my most important teachers will show up in my life.

Zalinda's is one of the most powerful stories of forgiveness that I have ever heard. It has made me look at my own belief system and the beliefs of our society. For example, as I look back at my past, I see that I was taught by my parents that there are some things in life that are just not forgivable. One of those things was most certainly murder.

While I was growing up I began to see that we live in a world where the majority of people believe that a great many things are simply unforgivable. If someone murdered your husband or child it would not only be considered abnormal for you to forgive him, but your forgiveness might even be considered insane. To forgive the murderer of someone you loved would seem appropriate grounds for you to see a psychiatrist.

Zalinda told me that in the beginning she had made it the number-one goal in her life to keep Michael, her son's murderer, in jail forever. There had been no question at all in her mind that what Michael had done was unforgivable. She spent all her time fanning the fire of her hatred and resentment. Every time Michael became eligible for parole, Zalinda was at the hearing with her family and friends doing everything they could to keep Michael in jail.

All the years that she did this, Zalinda felt that her emotions and behavior were both normal and appropriate. Then a few years ago she read one of my books, *Love Is Letting Go of Fear*, and she began to wonder about the value of continuing to live the rest of her life with her heart filled with hate and resentment.

Zalinda became a student of *A Course in Miracles*, a book that emphasizes spiritual transformation, forgiveness, peace of mind as our only goal, and learning to listen to the voice of God within each of us. Zalinda began to wonder if it would ever be possible for her to have peace of mind as her only goal rather than the hatred and vengeful feelings she had been hanging on to since her son's murder.

Zalinda began to do some of the daily workbook lessons in the *Course* about letting go of the past and not seeing value in guilt and blame. Although she experienced a lot of resistance, she continued to do the daily lessons and to do her best to listen to a voice within her heart that told her to start writing to Michael.

Zalinda began to argue with herself. She told herself, "Michael killed my son. He is my enemy. I don't want to have anything to do with him except to keep him in prison." But a gentle inner voice continued to instruct her to write to him, and she did. Reluctantly and shakily, she gave in to the voice.

Although I will go into more details a little later, what happened is that she later began to visit Michael. As these visits continued she began to look at him differently. She saw in him loving and caring qualities that allowed her to see that he had an identity beyond that of her son's murderer. With the realization of Michael's human qualities, a forgiveness process began. Zalinda began to do everything she could to help get him released from prison.

Needless to say, I was overwhelmed by Zalinda's

story. One of the first questions that came to my mind was, "If one of my sons was murdered, would I really be able to forgive his killer?" My honest answer is that I am not sure I could. I have serious doubts that I could do what Zalinda has done. I say this knowing that I have written many books about forgiveness and that I believe we can never have true peace of mind as long as there is anyone in our lives whom we have not totally forgiven.

Was I just fooling myself in the belief that total and continuous forgiveness is necessary for us to have peace within ourselves and in the world? When it came to personal issues, such as imagining my reaction if one of my sons were murdered, did my mind split itself off from my beliefs and become inconsistent?

Although Zalinda told me how much my teachings had helped her look at the world differently and learn what forgiveness was all about, in reading her letter that day I immediately knew that she had much more to teach me than I had to teach her.

I spoke with Zalinda on the phone several times and felt a persistant urging within my heart, telling me that I just had to meet with Zalinda and Michael. I wanted to feel the essence of their experience, to be there with them in person, to make it real for myself. I think I had to see Zalinda and Michael in person to quiet the "doubting Thomas" within myself and prove that this was really happening. So with Zalinda's help I made all the arrangements to fly to Boise, Idaho, and interview Zalinda and Michael at the Idaho State Penitentiary.

In the meantime, however, I had a monthly meeting at my home with the volunteers at our Center. I have a device attached to my phone that allows everyone in the room to hear the caller's voice. I made arrangements for Zalinda to call during this meeting and talk to the group. I thought she would make a marvelous teacher for everyone, but I didn't realize *how* impactful she would be.

That night there was a woman at the meeting, a former school administrator, who had become infected with AIDS through a blood transfusion. She was still filled with anger and hatred, blaming all homosexuals in the world for her AIDS. She listened to Zalinda's story with special interest and was so tremendously moved by what she heard that she began to look with new eyes at the unforgiving thoughts and grievances she had been hanging on to.

That night she was able to let go of her grievances, and the next day she wrote Zalinda a letter. She told Zalinda that her story had played an instrumental role in helping her to let go of her grievance toward homosexuals and to forgive. The hate that she had held in her heart vanished. This woman truly had a transformational experience through talking with Zalinda. She feels that she will never be the same again—a feeling that I must say I share with her.

Three weeks later I flew to Boise, Idaho. Zalinda met me at the airport and we drove together to the prison for our appointment with Michael. On the way, I asked if it would be all right with her if I spent an hour or so alone with Michael before she joined us. She willingly agreed.

My heart was filled with excitement as I anticipated this experience. As I had expected, there were the usual formalities and delays before being admitted into the prison. Then I was taken to the prison psychologist's office and was surprised to find it a fairly pleasant room, with comfortable furniture that gave one the feeling of friendliness and ease.

Michael, age thirty-five, came in looking a little tense and apprehensive. He was about five feet ten inches tall, slender, and wore a mustache. I told him how much I appreciated his agreeing to see me and asked him to tell me a bit about himself and his history.

"I was born in Los Angeles in 1954," he said. "I was nine months old when my parents moved to Pleasant Hill, California. I stayed there till I was about five years old, and then we moved to Walnut Creek, California. I went to school and was raised there until I moved to Idaho in 1976. At that time I was in the eighth grade and I had just started getting involved in drugs; marijuana at first, drinking, and then later I started getting involved in heavier drugs. By the time I was sixteen I was using heroin."

I asked, "Were you stealing to get money for the drugs?"

"Yes, I was stealing," he said. "Petty theft and stuff like that—credit card theft and burglaries. I got arrested for using a stolen credit card and was sentenced to six months in the county jail and five years probation. I later violated probation and was found in possession of a narcotic outfit—needle and everything—and was sent to the California Rehabilitation Center. I was released on seven years probation in January 1976 and came to Idaho. I stopped using hard drugs, but I continued to use alcohol.

"I was living with two other guys, and I drank real heavy. I never actually blacked out, but I was a pretty obnoxious, loud drunk. I didn't really know why I was drinking."

"Could you please tell me about the events that led up to the murder?" I asked.

"Well," he said, "we had just come back from a long trip and there were about six or eight of us who had been drinking. We had already killed off two bottles of rum and we decided to go to a bar. John Dorcheous, whom I had known since coming to Idaho, was a bouncer at this bar. We were there for a while and I was becoming obnoxious, as usual, drinking and carrying on.

"Well, I said something rude to one of the waitresses, and John came over and told me that if I said it again I would have to leave. I said it again, and he told me to leave. Then, just as I was leaving, I turned around real quick and hit him and knocked him out."

"What happened then?" I asked.

"The other bouncers were around, and they jumped on me and beat the living crap out of me. The cops came and John put me under citizen's arrest. On the way to the county jail they took me to the hospital to have my lip sewn up."

Michael went on, "I had enough money to bail myself out. I went to a Seven-Eleven to get a burrito, and then on the way back I decided to go over to John's house, who is my friend, and tell him that I was sorry for doing what I did. I thought that maybe the other bouncers might be there so I took my .32-caliber semiautomatic with me."

"What were your reasons for taking the gun?" I asked.

"In case they were there I thought I could pull the gun out and shoot a couple of bullets in the air and scare them enough to where they wouldn't want to beat me up again, and then I could beat a hasty retreat to my car.

"Of course, I was under the influence of alcohol and wasn't thinking clearly. This was just one in a long line of mistakes I made that night. I'm not trying to condone my actions or anything like that. The front door was open and I went in and I could hear John in the bedroom telling a friend, 'So I put him in jail.'

"I walked around into the room and said, 'Oh, so you put me me in jail, huh?' As John saw me, he jumped off his bed and said, 'I'll put you back in jail.'

20

"I fired my gun in the air twice as a warning. He came after me and we began to fight. He pulled off my glasses and hit my right hand, with the gun. As he grabbed my hand the gun went off, shooting him in the arm, chest, stomach, and head. He fell on top of me, and I just pushed him off of me, got up, and ran as fast as I could. I jumped in my car and drove all the way to Walnut Creek, California.

"The next day I decided to fly back to Boise, where I got a lawyer and turned myself in. I was sentenced for second-degree murder. They gave me a life sentence and a consecutive fifteen years for possession of a firearm while committing a felony."

"Michael," I said, "how did you deal with your own guilt, your self-esteem?"

"Well, that was the hardest part," he replied. "Like I said, I turned myself in. I had wanted to face up to what had happened, but I couldn't. I guess that I was in such a state at the time that I didn't really realize what I had done. And during the trial when I heard all this stuff coming out and what people were saying, I felt really bad. I didn't know how to deal with my guilt.

"I was so distraught that I thought I would never get out of prison. I thought that even though I might become eligible for parole they would never let me out."

"How did you try to deal with your guilt in prison?" I asked.

"I just suffered," was his reply. "There seemed to be nothing I could do about it. I have thought about committing suicide on a number of occasions. I had been in jail over nine years, without much hope of ever getting out, when Zalinda contacted me. I've been very much a loner in prison."

"Were you surprised when Zalinda said she wanted to visit you?"

"Yes, it was a complete surprise," Michael said. "My lawyer told me he had received a phone call from Zalinda saying that she wanted to visit me. He said that she was tired of all the hate and wanted to come out and meet with me. He advised me not to do so. But I said I would do it.

"Zalinda is on my regular visiting list now. I don't know how to put it in words, but when Zalinda came out and eventually forgave me for what happened . . . well, that just released the weight of the world from my shoulders. Later, I even began to think about the possibility of getting out and resuming my life."

At this point Zalinda joined us in the psychologist's office. I told her where we were in the interview and asked her if she could review the events that had led her to contact Michael.

Zalinda then told her side of the story: "My one wish in life had been for Michael to spend the rest of his life in prison. Whenever he was up for parole, I was there to block that from ever happening. As I began to read *Love Is Letting Go of Fear* and some of your other books, and *A Course in Miracles*, I began to realize that it was possible to look at things differently. I couldn't live the rest of my life with anger and pain. I chose not to do that anymore.

"It was a long process. I remember one time being in the courtroom at one of Michael's requests for a reduction of sentence. I was on the stand testifying, once again, why I thought the sentence should not be reduced. While testifying, I decided that this time I was going to look directly at Michael and try to make him feel uncomfortable. But Michael maintained eye contact with me, and that surprised me. Somehow, I thought he was trying to tell me he was sorry that this had all happened.

"My son Greg and I had written a letter stating that

we knew that Michael's parents had suffered and wanted him out as much as we wanted him in. As the hearing ended, I sensed Michael's parents behind me. I turned around and shook their hands and told them I had always known that they too were suffering, that it wasn't just our side of the family, and by this time we were all crying, and Michael's mother put her arms around me and gave me a hug and said that I had been in her prayers daily.

Following this there was that little voice within my heart that said, 'Forgive. Just do it!' I would spend a certain amount of energy arguing with myself, saying, 'You can't do this. Your family is going to think you're crazy. Your people are going to think you're nuts.' I just decided that I had to do this, regardless of how they felt."

I told her that it seemed to me that most people think it is sane to continue to hate someone and insane to choose to forgive and love. I then said to Michael, "This must have been the last thing in the world you would have expected . . . that the mother of the person you killed would come and ask if the two of you could work out a forgiveness process. Tell me what your reaction was when you heard this."

Michael replied, "Well, my first reaction was the same as my lawyer's. We both felt there must be an ulterior motive. I was scared to death. We didn't know what she had on her mind. There was some fear that maybe she was out to hurt me and get revenge. But it wasn't like that at all."

The remarkable letter that Zalinda sent to Michael on October 5, 1989, follows:

> Michael Kaiser,
>   After talking with Mr. Lynn [Michael's attorney] the other day I expect you will

not be surprised to receive these letters.

I honestly do not have a clear idea of how I want or expect an exchange between us to progress. The emotions are very intense and very real and painful. I will try to keep balance. John was my son and a very special person. I miss him in some way every day.

But for my own well-being and peace of mind I believe the time has come to try to reach a degree of forgiveness. So right up front I want you to know I am doing this for me. Somehow I think that to be able to talk with you would help me in this process. I cannot tell you what I want either of us to say, or even if I can reach any degree of forgiveness. I only know I feel strongly that this is the necessary next step.

Zalinda Dorcheous

I asked Zalinda what the first visit with Michael had been like, and she replied, "I was a nervous wreck. I made it clear to Michael that this visit was for me. I knew I had to honor my emotions. Although I didn't want to continue to hang on to hate and anger, I knew there was still a lot there. I was honest with my emotions and spent a good deal of time crying. I had a couple of questions that had been bothering me for years that I specifically asked Michael, and he answered them honestly."

One of those questions was, "Did John suffer?" Another: "Did he know what was coming?"

Zalinda went on to say, "There were times in that first meeting when there were silences because nobody knew for sure what to say. Then I began to visit him on a weekly basis."

As Zalinda continued to visit Michael in prison, she began a process of letting go of old images of him that she had been carrying. She began to see Michael in the present, without his past. As she talked about this change in the way she saw him, I couldn't help but think about the many, many ways that our egos make it so difficult for us to forgive.

There are two things that our egos want us to believe and will do everything in their power to convince us are true: The first is that there are some people in this world who do unforgivable things that deserve our hatred for the rest of their lives, and even after they are dead. The second is that if you do forgive, you will only get hurt again. Our egos want us to keep our anger hot and alive, not trusting, always on guard against the possibility of getting hurt again. It would have us believe that the past only repeats itself and that it is impossible to be truly peaceful in the present.

Zalinda, after many years of agony and resentment, had begun to change and to want peace of mind as her only goal. Although she wasn't sure that she was capable of forgiving, she was willing to forgive, and she kept giving her negative thoughts to her inner teacher, within her heart, to be transformed. She finally realized that she could not do this by herself.

Zalinda continued her story: "After going through this process with Michael, I have learned a lot because I was so filled with anger and pain, I never gave any time to thinking about how people in prison feel. I never gave time to think that they may have made serious mistakes but that they are also caring, sensitive, vulnerable people.

"Not only have I been able to see Michael differently, but I realize that there are many people in prison who could benefit from Attitudinal Healing and learning to share their feelings in an honest and open way.

Michael and I have shared a lot of our inner selves
with each other, and we have learned to trust and love
each other."

As Zalinda was talking, she and Michael were holding hands and tears were running down their cheeks.
Tears were also rolling down my cheeks as I saw
Zalinda, a mother whose son had been murdered,
looking only with tenderness and love into the eyes of
the man who had committed that murder.

There was a simplicity and purity in what I was
witnessing. I could not detect even a hint of animosity,
hate, or anger. Here we were, inside a state prison,
and the room was filled with peace and tranquility. It
is a picture that I will always have in my heart and will
never forget.

When I asked Michael about his forgiving himself
for the murder, he said, "I think to some degree I have
forgiven myself. I don't know if I will ever be able to
forgive myself completely. I'm still trying, and I think
with Zalinda's help I may be able to do it."

Zalinda then spontaneously interrupted: "Michael,
you know that I have forgiven you and no longer have
a problem with that. I can look at you now and not see
any of that old stuff. I just see you as the person you
are, right now."

I said to Zalinda, "I'm reminded of all those years of
anger and hate. You must never have dreamed that
forgiveness would ever be possible."

"Never in a million years," Zalinda replied. Michael
and I listened and were deeply moved as she told
how she had chosen the path of forgiveness. She
told how her readings and study of *A Course In Miracles* helped her to see that there just had to be another
way of looking at the world.

"I was destroying myself through my hate and bitterness. My body was falling apart, and it seemed to me

26

that all the hate inside me was attacking my own body. For example, my hair was falling out. I had bladder and gall bladder difficulties. I had a terrible rash on my hand that would not go away.

"Somehow I began to know inside me that if I was to survive forgiveness was not an option but a necessity. It was a struggle, because even thinking about forgiving Michael made me feel that I was being disloyal to my family and friends who had given me so much support. There was a bit of an argument going on inside me for a long, long time.

"After many months of visiting Michael, I began to see that he was not the cold, sadistic killer I once thought. He was a man who had *screwed up* because of drugs and alcohol. It became clear to me that he had commited a terrible error. But I also felt that he should be given a chance to go on with his life. My forgiveness was as much for me as it was for Michael. It was the only way I could survive."

That night I had dinner with Zalinda at the home of a mutual friend of ours. At one point during the dinner, our host remarked that Zalinda had been able to forgive Michael because she is an extraordinary person. I interrupted, saying, "No, no! That's the beauty of her story. I believe with all my heart that Zalinda is an ordinary person. The important thing is that what she *did* was extraordinary. And I think that's what gives me and other people hope that maybe we, too, can do what she did. She transformed her perception of Michael from an enemy into a friend. If I thought Zalinda was an extraordinary person, I think that would put a separation between her and myself and I would be tempted to say to myself that because she is extraordinary she could do that, but I am ordinary and that is beyond what I could ever do."

The next day as I was flying back to San Francisco

the image came back into my mind of Zalinda and Michael holding hands as friends. The thought occurred to me that if Zalinda could do that with someone who had murdered her son, then the rest of us ought to be able to heal whatever unhealed relationships we are holding on to.

Almost immediately a mental picture of a person whom I have known for many years, and still have an unhealed relationship with, came into my mind. Suddenly, without my doing anything, I felt a sense of total compassion and love toward this person that was beyond anything I could have ever imagined.

There I was on the plane with tears rolling down my cheeks, feeling a depth of peace and tranquility that was without limits. At that moment I knew that my relationship with this person was healed. It was a healing that part of myself feared would never be possible. More tears flowed, tears of release and tears of gratitude for Zalinda, who had taught me so much about forgiveness.

Since my visit to Idaho many things have happened. Zalinda came to Tiburon to attend an Attitudinal Healing Training Seminar because she is still interested in getting Attitudinal Healing Centers started in prisons. We, at our Center, are most eager to help her. She also spent much of her time doing everything she could to help get Michael released. Michael has written to me often, asking my help in getting him a job, and I'm doing everything I can to be of assistance.

At Michael's last parole hearing, Zalinda spoke on his behalf, and it was because of her testimony that Michael was released on July 17, 1989. On that momentous day of his release, Zalinda was there in her car to escort him out of prison, and there was a job waiting for him.

Afterword

Shortly after Michael was released from prison, *The Today Show* did a feature on Zalinda and Michael, and people were so impressed that Zalinda received several offers from movie studios to do her story.

For many years of my life, I had thought that total forgiveness could be applied only by a few very extraordinary people. In the world I saw, I had thought it was not only impossible but unsafe to forgive your enemies. Now I had proof that there truly is another way of seeing the world.

Zalinda's story demonstrates that the spiritual principle of forgiveness can be completely practical. Because of the stubbornness of our egos, it is often hard work and a never-ending process. For example, after she was told that Michael was going to be released, Zalinda called me on the phone and was honest enough to share the following with me:

"Jerry, my intial reaction was one of excitement and joy. It was the feeling of *it's about time, and it's about time for this ordeal to be over.* And then, to my surprise, I experienced some old feelings of resentment, anger, and revenge, and a momentary feeling of wondering if I had done the right thing. It didn't last long but I learned that forgiveness is a forever process. I know that I did the right thing, and I am at peace with my decision. I have learned how very important it is to release ourselves from the past."

I know that I have found a lifelong friend in Zalinda. It was not an easy decision for her and her son Greg to follow their beliefs and feelings, especially when it seemed to go against what their community and family believed and felt. Zalinda and Greg risked a great deal and they have led the way to a healing within their community and their family. Their story has also touched and helped to heal ever so many people outside their own family and community. I am delighted to share their story with others, knowing how it can help to heal us all.

CHAPTER

2

HENRI
LANDWIRTH

When I let all my grievances go,
I will know I am perfectly safe.

Henri Landwirth has been an extraordinary teacher for me, showing me that by helping others we can let go of the past and all the grievances that go with it. Although he faced challenges that most of us would find beyond our worst imaginings, Henri never gave up. His story is living proof that nothing is impossible, and there is a solution to any problem through love.

Before going on I would like to share with you an experience of my own that made Henri's story even more dramatic for me. In January 1989, I visited the place where his story began. That place was the Nazi concentration camp in Auschwitz, Poland, where thousands of Jews and gentiles died after enduring unthinkable torture during World War II. I really have no words to describe what I felt. That experience was one of the greatest shocks that I have ever experienced and I'm still in the process of absorbing what it means to me and attempting to sort it out. It remains a visceral experience that defies words.

I was there in the bitter cold of winter, wearing an overcoat, long underwear, a sweater, suit, coat, gloves, and a hat; and I was still cold. The guide who showed us through the prison camp told us that many prisoners had been clothed only in rags or had no clothes at all, even though the weather had been as cold as it was the day of my visit. I could not even imagine this, nor could I imagine the depth of the cruelty, fear, isolation, and feelings of abandonment that people suffered in this place, where more than six million people were put to their deaths. As I walked in and out of the buildings and across the same ground that literally millions of prisoners had walked, I couldn't help but ask myself, "If I had been here, could I have lasted for even one day?"

As I passed through the gate to the outside yard and walked along the dirt pathways between the barracks, my spine suddenly chilled as I realized how many thousands of people, much like me, had walked upon that ground I was walking. Unlike me, they had little to sustain them through painful hunger and the daily threat of torture and death.

The guide took us into one of the barracks that had been made into a museum. There were various rooms, each about the size of a large living room except that they had glass partitions in front of them. One room was filled with human hair that had been shaved from corpses to be woven into clothes.

A second room, about the same size, was filled high with metal orthopedic braces and canes. In a third room, I saw shoes of all sizes that had once belonged to men, women, and children, piled as high as the ceiling. In a fourth room there were stacks of suitcases with nametags still attached. In a fifth room were pictures of prisoners, both children and adults, in various stages of starvation. Many of them looked like skeletons with skin stretched over their bones. I had never imagined that human beings could stay alive with so little flesh on their bodies.

The guide took us into the barracks where the prisoners had slept. We saw wooden racks filled with straw, stacked one on top of another, where dozens and dozens of people had once been crammed in like sardines in a can. We were taken to see the dreaded "killing wall," located in a small courtyard, where thousands of prisoners had been lined up and shot, then carried away by fellow prisoners.

At one end of the prison yard was the so-called gas chamber, located underground. It was a large room, thirty by fifty feet, where people had been jammed in and killed by gas. Their bodies had then been carried into the next room to be incinerated, after the gold had been extracted from their teeth.

On the ground above the incinerator stood a huge, round metal chimney extending into the sky. When I saw this I was reminded of a businessman I know who is a survivor of the Holocaust. He once told me of this chimney and said that for many years he could not go by a factory with a chimney without imagining that he was smelling the odor of burning flesh.

Before the guide had finished showing us through the prison, my whole body began to ache. I felt filled to overflowing with sorrow, dismay, and horror such as I had never known. It was the worst and most painful experience I've ever had in my life.

As I write this, a month after my visit to the prison camp, I find that I am still in deep grief and sorrow. I find myself periodically weeping, both inside and outside, for those unfortunate souls who found themselves in the prison at Auschwitz and other concentration camps during World War II. But even as I felt myself sinking into a deep depression, another part of me knew that in the past I had always been provided with teachers who helped me see beyond my limited perceptions. The truth is that I had already been provided with a wonderful teacher and friend to help me in this. That man's name is Henri Landwirth.

Henri had been a prisoner at Auschwitz. As I thought about this, the question occurred to me that if I had been one of the few who did survive, like Henri, could I ever let go of my fear, anger, resentment, and grievances? Would I ever have been able to live a normal life? Would I ever have been able to experience trust and love? And would I ever dare take the risk of being giving and close to other people?

Old questions that I thought I had answered for myself began to pop up again. Once again I found myself asking, "Are there perhaps some things that people do in this world that are simply unforgivable? Are there some grievances that can somehow benefit us by holding on to them, by holding them dear to our hearts, as if they might shield and protect us from further harm?"

For the past fourteen years, as I traveled my spiritual pathway, I had come to believe that everything is forgivable and that there can never be any value in holding hate and anger in our hearts. Then, with this shaking experience of being in Auschwitz, I began to have real questions about my belief system. Perhaps, after all, I had been wrong. And in that moment I felt hate and anger filling my bloodstream, seeping into every single one of my cells.

At that moment, I remembered Henri, and as I thought about his life I began to let go of my grievances. Henri is a remarkable man who has become my dear friend, helping me, more than he realizes, to find another way of looking at the world. He has much to teach us all about the purpose of life and about healing. His determination allowed him to transform his pain and anguish into love and caring. He sheds light on a path that all of us can follow, where we no longer need to live in the past, holding on to bitterness and grievances, and shows us that it is possible to come to terms with the past and move beyond it, no matter how horrible it may have been.

As you'll see as you read Henri's story, he is a person who teaches by the way he lives, demonstrating that even when the most horrendous cruelty known to humankind has been committed, it is still possible to let go of fear, to let go of the past, and to put all one's energy into the present—giving, caring, and loving. Through Henri's example, those of us who have had painful pasts might find the guidance to let go of our grievances for what we have suffered, thus becoming free to commit ourselves totally to live, love, care for, and help one another in the present.

Diane Cirincione, my spiritual partner, and I met Henri in Florida in June 1988 when we were giving a lecture there. We were immediately drawn to him, and he to us. It was the beginning of a very warm and intimate relationship. Our friendship began with a feeling that we had known each other all our lives. It was almost as if we were long-lost brothers who had at last found each other again. Then, after he told us the story of his early life, I knew that I had to include him in this book.

At the time we met, Henri was sixty-one years old. He was born of Jewish parents in Antwerp, Belgium, on March 7, 1927. Henri is a handsome man with a wonderful smile. As I sat talking with him, I would never have guessed that he had suffered the hardships, fear, anguish, and loss that he would tell me about. Yet, he had. The early years of Henri's life are not pleasant to hear about. When he was still a child, Henri became a prisoner at Auschwitz and at several other Nazi concentration camps. I was horrified as Henri described the horrendous atrocities that he witnessed in these camps. The anger and anguish I felt were almost too much to bear. I did not want to believe that human beings were capable of inflicting such cruelty upon one another.

It has always been very difficult for me to imagine how anyone could go through the experience of being a prisoner in a concentration camp, and then go on with his life to become successful, trusting, caring, and loving. But I do know that I have received a miraculous sense of healing from knowing both Henri's story and what he has done with his life since those terrible years of his imprisonment. I share his story now not to focus on the brutality but to shine a light on the source of this man's generosity and the strength of his personal philosophy of giving and love.

When World War II broke out in 1941, I was sixteen years of age, still in high school, living in Long Beach, California. When I graduated in 1943 I had the good fortune of being accepted into the Naval V-12 program. Through this program, I received my education in medicine and later served as a corpsman at a naval hospital in California. During those years, Henri's life could not have been more different from mine.

In 1940, when Henri was thirteen years old, his family moved from Belgium to Poland, his father's native country. At the time, his father was a men's clothing salesman and they lived a very comfortable life. In recalling these years, Henri describes many wonderful memories of a close and caring family life. He remembers his mother as a very outgoing person, with tremendous energy and full of zest for life. His father and mother went dancing nearly every night.

"I had a wonderful mother and father," he told me. "There was a lot of closeness, a lot of love in our family."

Henri had a twin sister, Margot, and they were bonded in a special way. It was the magnetism of this loving bond that later served as the source of a powerful determination that would bring them back together after a long separation caused by the war.

Henri told me that one day his father came home from work and announced that the Germans were coming to occupy Poland. He told his family that their lives were in danger and that they must escape from Europe to save themselves.

"I have a way to get out of Europe through Russia and then go on to China," Henri's father said.

His mother answered, "As long as I have my bed and my family is together, I want to stay."

Soon after, the Germans arrived. Within a short time, Henri's father was arrested and taken to prison. His family never saw him again, nor did they learn what had happened to him until many years later, when Henri discovered that his father had been shot and killed only a short time after his arrest.

A few months after his father was taken away by the Nazi soldiers, Henri was taken to the concentration camp at Auschwitz. He was a very strong boy, about fourteen years old at the time, and so was valued for his ability to work. As he told me this part of the story, I recalled my own life during those same years. While I was entering high school in Los Angeles, Henri was entering an insane world where childhood and adolescence abruptly disappeared.

Henri was not alone. Thousands of other children were sent to the camps, many of them much younger than he. No words can possibly describe the depth or the degree of pain, suffering, and loss that were experienced by so many children suddenly being separated from their parents in this way. As they were separated, few knew if their mothers and fathers, brothers and sisters, relatives and friends were still alive. Nor did they know if they would themselves be alive another day. They suddenly found themselves in a world where everything they had ever known about trust, faith, and love was being challenged as it had never been challenged before.

As we went on with the interview, Henri paused many times, telling me that he simply could not find the words to describe the conditions of the camps.

"Many things I don't remember," he said. "But I do remember the smell of the crematoriums at night. I remember the beatings and hangings and people dying of hunger and disease all around me. The biggest problem was the terrible hunger and thirst we experienced. Being hungry is one of the worst feelings that a human being can have."

As Henri talked, I felt my adrenaline rising. My stomach felt like a rope that was being tied into a mass of impossible knots. A part of me wanted to shut out what he was telling me about man's inhumanity to man. Another part of me was listening with great intensity, wanting to discover how this man had been able to live through challenges that I would have thought impossible.

"From Auschwitz I was taken to an even worse camp," Henri continued. He told of an underground camp where he and his fellow prisoners were forced to work in a factory producing anti-aircraft guns. There were about two thousand prisoners in all. They slept on springs without mattresses. In this prison they were treated worse than the lowest of animals.

"They made us run ten miles every day, almost nude, or with hardly any clothes on our backs. They tortured us in many ways." Henri stopped for a moment. He did not describe the ways he and his fellow inmates were tortured; I had a feeling that this was a subject he could not discuss with me.

"From the camp where we produced weapons, we were sent to Guushen 2, which was even worse,"

Henri continued. "Then I was taken to an underground camp close to Dresnow, Germany. I had no idea where I was because all the time I was there I did not see light, the sun, or anything outside the prison at all.

"Many prisoners died of typhoid, and sometimes prisoners who were well took the leftover food rations of those who were very ill, even though they knew they would probably get sick from typhoid if they ate this food. They ate it anyway, just for the sake of feeling full for once."

As I listened to Henri's story, I found myself wondering if I, at age thirteen, would have been able to cope with being separated from my parents and taken to prison. What was there in Henri that allowed him to survive when so many around him were dying? Perhaps one thing that gave him strength was his unwavering hope and absolute determination to be rejoined eventually with his family.

Toward the end of the war, an underground movement developed in the camp where Henri was being held prisoner. One day some men who were involved in it asked Henri to "make a mistake" that would sabotage the anti-aircraft weapons he was being forced to work on. The plan was that after doing this, Henri would eat some typhus-infected food; the Germans then would send him to the hospital, where he would be rescued by people from the underground. He agreed to the plan.

"The only time we were ever sent to the hospital was in the very last hours of our lives," Henri explained.

He ate the typhus-infected food and quickly became very ill. With a seriously high fever, he felt like he was in a trance.

"I was taken to the hospital," he said, "and in the middle of the night, when I didn't know where I was or what I was doing, somebody came in and gave me something to drink."

The next morning, when he awoke, Henri found himself surrounded by dead people. He was the only person alive in that room. Somehow he had survived, only to be returned to the prison camp.

"After that," Henri said, "I was never fully normal. Many of my friends died, and I was encouraging everybody to run away. 'Come, let's run away!' I told them. 'Why should they just kill us here? We might as well get killed running.' "

With Russian and American troops closing in, the camp where Henri was a prisoner became a target, since it was known to be a munitions factory. Both prisoners and German soldiers died during the Allies' shellings, and finally, with only three hundred of the original two thousand prisoners still alive, the Germans decided to evacuate. The soldiers marched the prisoners on foot for two days until they came to a large barn.

Henri kept telling the other prisoners, "Let's run away! Let's escape!"

A German soldier overheard him. "He hit me over the head with the butt of his rifle," Henri said. "Covered with blood, I burrowed into a pile of straw and lost consciousness. When I awoke, all the other prisoners were gone. The Germans had left me for dead, but then the soldiers recaptured me and took me to still another prison.

"It was a terrible prison," Henri recalled. "Rats and mice were all over the place. Water was running from pipes and I was hoping at the time that death would come to me because I couldn't stand it anymore.

"After a few days I was taken out of the prison to a place outside this little town. I don't know where it was. There were many soldiers, and there were two other prisoners with me. I understood and spoke German, and one of the soldiers said to me, 'We have orders to kill you, but the war is almost over. Line up facing the woods and when we pick up the guns you start running.' This was a true miracle because the soldiers who had been given orders to shoot us let us get away.

"I traveled on foot for many weeks, sleeping in churches and attics, and stealing food to eat. My feet became infected with gangrene and I was in terrible pain. I was scared to go to a doctor because I was afraid I would be recaptured and killed. I wasn't really normal. I wasn't aware of my fear; it was as though I had absolutely none. I was in a crazy state."

Henri ended up in a town in Czechoslovakia where he found a deserted house to sleep in. A woman found him there and told him, "The war is over. Where are you going?"

Henri remembered telling the woman, "I can't stop. The war isn't over."

The woman convinced Henri that it was safe to come across the street to her home. It was there that she turned on the radio so that he could hear the news that the war really had ended.

The woman's husband gave Henri a bath—the first one he had had in many months—and they nursed him back to health. When he was well enough to leave he went to Krakow, Poland, to find out about his family. There was a center in Krakow for former prisoners of war. They were given food there and exchanged information about what had happened to their families and friends.

Henri was given a job in a dentist's office, where he also had a place to sleep. Every day during his lunch hour he would go to the center to exchange news about his relatives and friends. One day on the trolley car, he saw a woman who looked familiar to him, although he didn't know her name or where he had seen her before. When she got off at the next stop he automatically got off behind her and started following her down the street.

He called to her, asking her to stop. "I want to know who you are," he said.

"If you don't stop following me," the woman replied, "I will call the police."

"Please tell me who you are," Henri begged.

"No! Get away from me," she insisted.

Without knowing why, Henri called out his mother's name and the woman stopped in her tracks. She turned around and let Henri catch up with her. Then they stood and talked for a long time. The woman's name was Mrs. Zawuska, and she had been Henri's mother's best friend before the German occupation of Poland.

As Henri told me this, I could not help but think that love must surely have a memory bank that can never be erased. It must be that the love we experience in our lives creates a light that can never be put out. And when we tap the source of that love, miracles occur in our lives that are beyond our intellectual understanding. Henri's story teaches us that when we focus on the love in our hearts, with the intensity of a laser beam, as he must have done, limitations fade away and even the impossible comes true.

The next day a chauffeured limousine arrived at the dentist's office where Henri lived and worked. The driver went to the door and asked for Henri.

"Mr. and Mrs. Zawuska would like you to come to their house," the driver said. "Bring your things, because you're going to stay with them."

Henri went with the chauffeur to the Zawuska's home. When they realized how sick he was, they saw to it that he received the best medical care. As his health improved, Henri became aware of the fact that he didn't even know how to eat at the table. Having spent four years in the very worst prison camps, he had completely lost his sense of manners.

When his health was finally restored, Henri set out to find any surviving members of his family. He discovered that his mother had been put aboard a ship with two thousand other women just a few weeks before the war ended. The ship was sent out to sea and deliberately blown up. Everyone aboard was killed.

Grief-stricken by the news of his mother's death, Henri learned that his sister might be living with several other women in a little town in Germany. He set out on foot to find her, walking and hitchhiking many hundreds of miles.

"One morning," he said, "I ended up in the small town where I had been told I might find my sister. I asked everyone I met if they knew anything about her. Finally I met someone who said there was such a woman, and he told me how to find the house where she lived.

"When we were children, my sister and I had a special way to whistle when we wanted to call each other," Henri explained with a smile. "I stood outside the house where I had been told I might find her and whistled in that way. After a while, a man came out and asked me what I wanted. I told him I was looking for my sister, Margot.

" 'There is no woman named Margot here,' the man said."

Henri remembered that when he and his sister were very small they had special names for each other. She called him Didek and he called her Doda. He asked the man if he knew a woman called Doda, and he did!

Henry described his wonderful reunion with his sis-

ter. He was overjoyed at being with her again. He
could not remember a time when he had been so
happy. He told me, "This was surely a miracle!"

Once again I thought how the power of love knows
no limits or boundaries. It has a wonderful energy that
cuts through all obstacles. When we tap into and trust
the energy of love that is always active in our hearts,
we find that we have the power to resolve all our
problems and difficulties.

After their reunion, Henri and his sister decided to
go to the United States. Many, many months passed
before they could get the proper papers, and during
that time his sister was married and became pregnant.
Henri, his sister, and her husband went to Belgium,
where her baby was born.

While in Belgium, Henri learned how to be a diamond cutter. Then, in 1950, he emigrated to the United
States with only twenty dollars in his pocket. At first
he worked as a diamond cutter, but only a short time
after arriving he was drafted into the army.

He served two years in Korea, after which he went to
school in New York City to learn hotel management.
He was married in 1954 and went to Florida on his
honeymoon. He and his wife liked Florida so much
that they stayed, and this is where he lives to this day.

"As soon as I moved to Florida things started to turn
around for me in a big way," he explained. "I became
the manager of a luxury hotel and met many wonderful people, from the poorest on up to dignitaries. I
managed Holiday Inn hotels, and in 1969 I got a franchise for a Holiday Inn at Disney World." Henri now
owns a 672-room luxury hotel at Disney World and is
planning to build another one.

As he finished telling me his story, I thought a lot
about the difficulties Henri had conquered. I had to
ask him the following question:

"Of all the terrible experiences that you've had in your life, what was the worst?"

"The hunger," Henri said. "Nothing can be worse than hunger. You cannot explain hunger. You have to experience it. Once you do, you will find out what hunger is. In the concentration camps, all of us were just waiting for death. So, the hunger was something that was constantly on our minds. When you are hungry, you can think of nothing else, and the animal instincts take over."

I want to emphasize that Henri has chosen not to go through life embittered by the horrendous experiences of his early years. Rather, he has chosen to see himself as living on very precious "borrowed time." He chose not to live a life in which he was constantly reliving the past, but to do his best to live in the present.

He is now living a life of deep gratitude, believing that his purpose is to embrace the world, to make it a better place, and to demonstrate how one person can make a difference by giving to others who are in need. Giving has become a way of life, a way of saying thank you to God for life.

At the time of my original interview with him, Henri had just announced that he had turned over the management of his hotel business to other people in order to devote more of his time to his work in the world peace movement.

He is the founder of an organization called Give Kids the World, the function of which is to help children who have catastrophic illnesses and are facing the possibility of death. Give Kids the World brings these children and their families to Disney World and pays for their lodging, food, and all other expenses.

In Henri I see a man who intuitively knows that the bleeding scars of his past can be healed not by dissecting and analyzing them, but by living in the present and making his life purpose helping and loving others. He is a valuable teacher, showing us all that by helping and loving others, the constrictions around our hearts begin to disappear and our hearts expand. What once might have seemed like empty holes in our hearts, holes that could never be filled, become healed and filled with love simply by giving our love to others. For me, his life has been an inspiring example of how much there is to learn about faith, determination, and hope.

In 1988, Henri decided to build his own village at Disney World where the children and their families could stay free of charge. Care has been taken to build wheelchair ramps and to offer provisions for other special needs the kids have. It is an oasis of hope, joy, and relaxation for these families. The many letters that Henri has received from the families that have come to the village are more than enough proof of the tremendous value of his generous endeavors.

I know how much this work means to the children who come to the village. I first heard about Henri through a volunteer at the Center for Attitudinal Healing in Tiburon, California, where we work with children and their families facing catastrophic illness and the possibility of death. The volunteer told me about a newspaper article she'd seen about Henri and she suggested that I telephone him to see if one of our children could go to his Children's Village at Disney World.

Through our children at the Center for Attitudinal Healing, I have become very much aware of the pains, tribulations, and sorrows these families face. People like Henri Landwirth and organizations like Give Kids the World are truly a godsend for these children. For these families in their time of need and distress, it is like a gift from heaven to be offered boundless love, free lodging, food, and a trip to Disney World.

Henri gives generously of his time and money to other projects as well, including a program to help homeless people and to feed the hungry. In addition, he has been actively involved in helping the elderly and has built a facility in Orlando. He is always on the lookout for new ways in which he might be helpful to others.

I asked Henri if he was able to put his life purpose into words. He immediately replied, "Number one, I want to give back. I have a tremendous desire to give back. My life has been fulfilled in many, many different areas. For many years I had no sense of purpose. Now I'm beginning to see a lot of things. The important things in life are just coming to the surface for me."

As we talked, it struck me what a remarkable example he is of the principle that nothing is impossible. He exemplifies this not only by having survived the horrors at Auschwitz but by becoming very successful in the hotel business and using his money to serve others.

Henri has also been a teacher of humility because many of the things he does, he does in such a quiet and gentle way. He is the kind of person who prefers to stay in the background. It is clear that it is not recognition he is after. Yet, in 1989, in recognition for his contributions to humanity, many of which will never be made public, he was chosen "one of the twelve most caring individuals in the United States" by the Institute for Caring, in Washington, D.C. His focus in life is not on money but on giving to and helping others. From the depths of his being, in both his personal philosophy and his actions, Henri views giving as an important part of his own healing.

Henri has an uncanny ability to focus on whatever project he is working on. Not even the smallest detail slips by him. In his work for world peace, personal thank-you notes go out to everyone who has joined him in his cause. Perhaps one of the reasons why Henri was able to survive the concentration camps is that he learned to be extremely focused on the present. Today, rather than holding on to the pain of his past, he has chosen to let go of that pain and to make use of what he learned in those awful days of suffering.

Throughout the ages, it has been said over and over again that everything that happens to us in our lives, no matter how painful or traumatic, can be turned into a positive lesson. In my study of *A Course in Miracles*, I found a sentence that means much to me: "All things are lessons that God would have us learn."

It seems to me that Henri demonstrates this principle very clearly in his life. He could have spent the rest of his life, as many people have, being bitter and seeing himself as an innocent victim. He chose, however, not to see himself as a victim or to make an idol of his pains from the past. With hard work and concentration, he kept a vision of himself as successful.

As Henri continued his story, he made it clear that his financial success was not the final goal of his life at all. In fact, he had discovered that his financial success did not bring him true happiness; rather, the balance he needed was inner success. He began to find that he experienced spiritual fullness only from caring and giving love to others. Henri teaches us that true joy doesn't really come from getting things; nor does it come from revenge. It comes from that burning desire to be helpful to other souls who are hurting and who are crying out for help.

At this point in the interview, I asked Henri about his children. He told me that he has three—Gary, Greg, and Lisa. One is a veterinarian, another an auditor, and a third works for the Big Brothers and

Big Sisters organization. I asked Henri if he had ever discussed his war experiences with his children.

"No," he replied, "I have not talked about my war experiences with anyone. The things I shared with you today, I don't believe I ever shared with anyone."

When I asked Henri how much his Auschwitz experience pained him, he replied, "I will never forget it. When I was released from the concentration camp, I was full of hate. Today I don't have any hatred and I believe this comes from my doing my best to concentrate on living in the present and giving to others. This helps me to not relive the past.

"I still think of my parents a lot. And when I do the pain of what happened to them still becomes my pain. I feel somehow I am living on borrowed time, and that time is not to be spent with hate but in caring and giving to others."

At about the time Henri and I were getting to know each other, I was holding monthly meetings in my home with a group of people who as children had been prisoners in concentration camps. Many of them, like Henri, had not shared with their children their personal experiences during the Holocaust.

I felt that these people kept their painful memories locked up in a vault in their minds because they were afraid that if they talked about the past, they would re-experience more pain than they could bear.

Now, however, many of these people have begun to share their experiences with their children. They have concluded that for them to experience inner peace, they needed to take their pain out of the vault, to process it, honor it, and then to let it go. A number of these people are now on spiritual pathways, devoting their lives to giving to and helping others.

As I thought about that, I said to Henri, "It might be

a gift for your children for you to tell them about your years in the Nazi camps."

Henri gave this some thought, then replied, "I don't know why I haven't shared, but I pushed it back in my mind. I just felt that I wanted to have a normal life and look to today and tomorrow and forget about the past."

He paused. "The problem is, our generation is dying out. I've done a lot of things to let the world know about the war. I have even been involved with funding a grant for educational films on the Holocaust."

Some time after this interview I had an opportunity to view some of the films he had helped to finance. I thought they were excellently done. Although there are many different things that a viewer may get out of these films, the number one thing that I got was the critical importance of never letting ourselves become so immobilized with fear that we develop a state of apathy toward what is going on around us. The films made me want to be more aware of human injustices in the world, and to take an active role in doing something about them. The films also made me want not to be guilty of near-sighted vision, but always to have a global vision and a willingness to help others.

· Today there is an inner joy in Henri that escaped him most of his life. I asked him if making money had gotten in the way of his being able to see his purpose earlier in life.

"Well, the money is wonderful, too," he said. "As long as you use it right . . . I like to have the money so that I am able to do all these other things I want to do. I do not join any other organizations or give money to groups. Most of my giving is single-handed, without people knowing.

"My goal is to find peace, to find tranquility. Too often I am always running, and I am too critical and upset. I hope I can find some peace; I'm searching for that and feel at long last I'm beginning to find it."

"You mentioned miracles that happened to you, both in Germany during the war and here," I said. "Do you think miracles have something to do with God?"

"Well," Henri answered, "I believe there is a God. I don't know what that is, but I believe in God and I believe in faith. I have always been a great believer in faith. In my own way of thinking, what has happened to me is what I will call faith. It is meant for me to be here. It is meant for me to do all these things."

I then asked, "Is it like God's plan—is that another way of putting it?"

"That's right," Henri replied. "I believe in that. I also believe that for me to be here, I consider myself living on forty-three years of borrowed time, and that is God's will. I am living on borrowed time today."

I then asked, "Many, many years from now, after you have died, suppose there is a stone on your grave, and there is one sentence on that stone to tell about your life. What would you want that sentence to say?"

Henri replied, "I would like it to say that he did his very best to bring peace and love into the world."

Afterword

In February 1989, Henri's organization, Give Kids the World, sponsored a delegation of thirteen to come from the Soviet Union to Disney World. Four children with catastrophic illnesses came with their mothers; one of the children was accompanied by his grandmother. This was done with the cooperation of the Center for Attitudinal Healing and Children as Teachers of Peace.

When I was in Poland in 1989, I had met an eight-year-old boy with leukemia. I asked Henri about giving the boy a trip to the United States; three months later, another miracle of joy took place as the boy and his mother came to Disney World as guests of Give Kids the World. And so the giving continues.

Henri Landwirth is a teacher to all of us, demonstrating that it is possible to let go of the past, that we can let go of hate, anger, revenge, and bitterness. He is an exceptional example of the amazing capacity of the human heart to deal with the gravest of all hardships and still go on, when we have faith.

Most of us in this world, thank God, have not had to go through the kinds of experiences that Henri did. Yet, many of us continue to believe that we must hang on to our grievances and live lives that are centered upon our own needs. Henri teaches us that no matter what the pain, no matter what the grievance, it is always possible to learn to let go.

He also points out that the way of self-healing is to love and care for others. He is a living example of how a life focused on giving in the present is a way to give hope to others as well as ourselves. Henri has discovered that true joy comes to the heart that is willing to be helpful, tender, and loving to those in need, to those who are crying out for help because they are suffering from fear and lack of love. Henri spends his time living in the present, and he does his best to resist analyzing the past.

We all have much to learn from Henri. I hope that each person who reads Henri's story will be given new strength to look at his or her pain and suffering and then, like Henri, to let go of the grievances and bitterness and to transform even what might seem the most negative experiences into compassion, caring, giving, and loving.

I have learned so much through my friendship with Henri that it is very difficult for me to list what he has taught me in any logical order. I do believe that we learn much from each other, not just from biographical details, but from the essence of the person him- or herself, which is in the spaces between the details and which no words can describe.

If Henri can let go of his past, then there is much hope that you and I can let go of our pasts. Henri's life story reminds me how important it is to look into my past to see if I am still holding on to painful memories, rather than loving ones, and to make the decision to live in the present, totally committed to love.

Henri teaches us that learning is a continuous process. He now knows that he is going in the right direction, and he has learned that even an attack can be a call for help and love. He knows that giving and receiving are the same. He no longer has to have a barrier to protect his heart and he does not have to keep his heart closed out of fear. Most important, he no longer has to be fearful of love.

The lesson and message for all of us who are still walking around with injured, seemingly irreparably broken hearts is that our hearts are never empty. The more unconditional love we give to others, the more whole and healed our hearts become.

The final lesson Henri's life teaches us is that nothing is impossible.

I do not know anyone who works harder than Henri as he pursues his goal to help children who are facing life-threatening diseases. Through his efforts, hundreds of children have had a reprieve from the tedium of their illnesses and have been able to experience happiness and joy. Henri is doing his utmost to open his heart and to follow a spiritual path. In the past, he may have been known as a workaholic, but I think that he is rapidly becoming a "heartaholic." Another thing that impresses me about Henri is that he does so many kind things for other people to make their lives a little happier, but he keeps his works a secret. His efforts have benefited many people who never knew the name of the angel who extended himself to them.

Because of Henri's experiences at Auschwitz, it is easy to understand why he may have felt, at times, that he had to have a tough heart. What I see today in Henri is a man who is allowing himself to be vulnerable—allowing his tender and gentle heart to shine. The light he sends out into the world around him is truly making a difference.

3

WALLY "FAMOUS" AMOS

Nothing but your own thoughts
can hamper your success.

Wally Amos is a wonderful teacher who gives people hope that nothing is impossible and that each of us can make a difference. He teaches that when you believe in yourself totally and are totally committed to helping others, everything becomes possible.

In the beginning of his life, Wally faced many hardships and challenges. Yet, he has been able to transform the experiences of those early years into positive lessons, which has helped him to become successful in his life and to become a great inspiration for us all. He managed to start his own business and to become president of Famous Amos Chocolate Chip Cookies, which are now found throughout the world. He came from a poor and dismal background, and he speaks with authenticity to the many people from similar backgrounds who see him as a model.

Early in our friendship, Wally became interested in the work at our Center for Attitudinal Healing. He has given generously of his time, talking with children who have catastrophic illnesses through our telephone support network. Every time I have asked him to phone some child or visit a family, he has been quick to respond. And of course he always sends them his "calling card"—his famous chocolate chip cookies. He not only visits or phones these children, he keeps up his friendships with them and their families, frequently for many years.

For example, eight years ago I put Wally in touch with a twelve-year-old child named Kerry, who had sickle cell anemia and had come close to death many times. Wally not only called him but still visits him every time he goes to Atlanta. This boy is now nineteen years of age; he is a pre-med student and wants to become a pediatrician so he can help others. Wally continues to give Kerry love, support, and a belief in himself.

Wally also became friends with young Derek Schmidt, who had leukemia and died from that disease. Derek had great faith in God and it was wonderful for him to have a friend like Wally, who has a similar faith in God but can also be natural, humorous, and even silly. Wally brought a tremendous amount of joy not only into Derek's life but into Derek's parents' lives as well.

I believe Wally is on the phone more than anyone I know saying, "Aloha, this is Wally!" which always brings a message of happiness and joy. Although Wally is not a minister, I've always felt that he has a ministry on the phone, always calling people at exactly the time when they are feeling low and in need of an uplifting call.

If ever there was a man out to make people happy, to put a smile on their faces and to make it a lighter day for them, to reach out a helping hand, to commit himself to be directed by God, it is Wally. He works as hard and as consistently as anyone I know to help others as part of his spiritual path.

In Wally's office is a sign that I will never forget: A VOLUNTEER IS SOMEONE WHO REACHES THEIR HAND INTO THE DARKNESS TO HELP ANOTHER HAND OUT INTO THE LIGHT ONLY TO DISCOVER IT IS THEIR OWN. It reminds me that to give is to receive. By helping others we help ourselves. These are truths that Wally demonstrates in his life every day.

I first met Wally Amos when I was giving a lecture in Hawaii at Unity Church in Diamond Head in 1979. I had brought some children with me from our Attitudinal Healing Center in Tiburon, California, who were suffering from catastrophic illnesses. Wally and his wife Christine were in the audience. They came up afterward and introduced themselves. Not only did they want to thank us for the lecture, but they wanted to offer free chocolate chip cookies for our annual picnic. A few weeks later, after we'd returned to California, we received several cartons of cookies. To me it was like receiving cartons of gold.

I had been addicted to Wally's chocolate chip cookies for years, so it was a delight to meet him and Christine at last. Little did I realize that we would become the closest of friends. Since that first meeting, I don't think a week has gone by without our talking on the phone.

Today millions of people know Wally's name and have seen a picture of his happy, smiling face. Many have read his books or seen him on television. In this chapter I'd like to tell you a little about the man behind that face.

Wally is the national spokesperson for Literacy Volunteers of America, and he devotes much time to help create opportunities for people to learn to read and write. He spends countless hours on this project and has helped many people in prison become motivated to learn to read.

Many times I have seen him face crises in his life, but never have I seen him express even one bit of self-pity. Almost the first words out of his mouth when he meets another person are, "What can I do to be helpful to you?"

There have been times when I felt that I was sinking in quicksand, and then there was Wally calling me on the phone just at the right moment, to be there to love and support me. There is little question in my mind that Wally knows that the key to his own peace, his own salvation, is helping others. If you would ever want a model of a tireless volunteer who never gives up, it would be Wally.

Many awards and honors have been bestowed on Wally, not the least of which was the Horatio Alger award. He has received an honorary Doctorate in Education from Johnson and Wales University, the President's Award for Entrepreneurial Excellence, and many others.

Wally is now fifty-three years old. In our interview the first thing I asked him was, "Will you tell me about the house where you grew up and about your early life?"

Wally replied, "We lived in Tallahassee, Florida, in a little house right on the railroad tracks. It was at the height of segregation, whites on one side, blacks on the other. Even growing up in that environment I was never bitter or had any anger toward whites.

"My mom was a domestic and my dad a common laborer. Dad wasn't around very much, and Mom was pretty tough. She was the disciplinarian. She would hit you with anything—switches or extension cords. My folks were divorced when I was twelve years old. My mom then went to Orlando, Florida, to live with her sister and her mom, and I moved to New York City to live with her other sister, Aunt Della. A year later my mom came to New York and I started living with her again and my grandmother Julia. In New York I delivered papers, worked on an ice truck, in a dairy, and in a supermaket."

"Wally," I asked, "what was the worst experience you had with your mom?"

"I had a tremendous fear of her. I would admit to that. I remember one time when I had some money that she had given me to pay the telephone bill and I lost the money shooting pool. Well, I knew I couldn't go home that night because my mother would probably kill me. So I rode around on the subway all night. The next morning at school they called me to the office. I went home crying and apologizing and saved myself a beating.

"I was never really a bad kid but my mother had me toe such a line that if I went either to the left or right of it, that was enough for her to beat me. When I was a kid growing up in Florida, she would sometimes beat me until there were welts on my back and my bottom. But you know, I have worked through a lot of that. I told her some years ago, 'Ruby, if you were raising me today I would have you arrested for *child abuse.*' "

Wally's mother is now eighty years old. Wally is quite attentive to her, phoning her weekly and visiting her whenever he's in Los Angeles. I asked, "Do you think you've been able to forgive your mom?"

"As a kid, I didn't question her authority," Wally replied. "From the time I was a baby, that was the way she raised me and I accepted that. But now I know that it had an effect on our relationship for a long time. It also had an effect on my relationships with everybody else, especially the other females I came in contact with.

"Because I wasn't raised in a loving environment and was unable to express myself, I couldn't share love with anyone because it had never been shared with me. I had to really look at that and work through a lot of forgiveness. I had to realize that my mother was just doing what she had been taught. Her mother had beat up on her, too."

"Wally, how did you deal with your own anger?"

He replied, "I wasn't ever an angry kid. The kids used to pick on me because I was skinny. They would get angry at me because I'd never fight back. I was never a fighter and just never expressed anger."

"What about your dad?" I asked. "What was he like?"

"He was a quiet guy although he and my mom used to fight all the time. They would start yelling and hitting each other. I never knew what it was about. They really got at it with each other.

"My dad worked at the natural-gas plant, shoveling coal, tending the furnaces, doing whatever they told him to do. I never really got to know what he was like inside. We never sat down and talked about who we were. He passed away a couple of years ago. He had moved to New York and I used to visit him occasionally, but we never really felt close."

Wally has had two marriages, and it's been very difficult for him to know how to be a loving father to his three sons because he had no model with whom he could identify. He neither spent much time with nor felt much love from his father, and his childhood home was filled more with anger and fear than with love.

It's no wonder that Wally and thousands of other men and women from similar backgrounds have found it so difficult to experience love. Never having experienced love as children, and never feeling they had the capacity for love, they feel unlovable. For many years it seemed to Wally that women were dangerous enemies. This was likely because he had not really completed his unfinished business in terms of his feelings toward his parents.

I next asked, "What kind of religious upbringing did you have?"

Wally replied, "My father was a Baptist and my mother a Methodist. I had a little bit of all of that. I was very religious. I would go to church on Sundays and attend Wednesday night prayer meetings. It was all about Hell and damnation. I would go to the services and I was supposed to all of a sudden feel God, or the Holy Ghost.

"Well, for a long time I didn't feel anything. I was one of the last kids to get religion. I kind of decided that I was going to get religion because everybody else had it. So I would be running and shouting all over the place, and that was the sign that I had gotten religion. When you got religion you got baptized in a lake or out in the woods. Then as I got older I got away from religion and the church.

"It wasn't until many years later that I began to experience God in a totally different way in the Unity Church in Hawaii. I started going to Unity in 1978. During those intervening years I was pretty self-centered and me-oriented. I was about as controlling and manipulative as you could get. I didn't know it then, but I really felt unlovable, fearful of love, and fearful of God."

"Have you ever had some kind of sudden transformation experience, an experience where you felt God's Presence?" I asked.

"In 1974, I took my three kids with me to the Grand Canyon, then on up to the Rocky Mountains and to Denver. Sitting on the rim of the Grand Canyon, I really went through a transformation. I had never been in awe of anything before, and I had never seen anything so magnificent in my life. I experienced the peace of God like I had never experienced anything before. But being on a spiritual pathway and devoting myself to service did not come to me like a bolt of lightning from the sky. On the contrary, it's been a very gradual process.

"I joined the Unity church in Hawaii and a short

time later I met Christine. These two events were certainly the most meaningful of my life. They were real turning points.

"I eventually became a member of the Board of Directors of the Church, and the friendships that developed with people I met there provided some of the most rewarding experiences I've had."

I asked Wally to tell me what happened after he left home.

"I dropped out of high school to join the Air Force. After I got out I worked at Saks Fifth Avenue and then worked for the fire department. Later on I worked for the Willam Morris Agency, which at that time was looking for a black trainee.

"I first got married in 1958, to Maria. Michael and Gregory came out of that marriage. It was terminated in 1962. As I look back I can see I was very selfish and egotistical; everything had to be the way I wanted it to be. I fooled around a lot and was not very loving. I didn't have a clue about how to really love. It wasn't until years later that I began to see how I was raised to make commitments to jobs but not to personal relationships.

"My second marriage, to Shirley, was in 1967. There were many separations and then a divorce about five years later. My son Shawn was a product of that marriage.

"I continued to have trouble with personal relationships. As soon as we had sex I would be looking to get away from the relationship and go somewhere else. I never wanted to give a part of me to any relationship, and it wasn't until my relationship with my present wife, Christine, that I began to see that here was someone who really, really loved me. How many people can say that in a lifetime? And, as you know, we now have Sarah, who is five and a half years old.

"Jerry, for the first time in my life, after I met Christine, I knew I'd met a person who totally loved me and accepted me as I was. How blessed I have been to have met a person who is so totally able to give me unconditional love, to help me accept myself, to help me forgive myself and heal my past, and to join me as a life partner in doing God's work. From Christine I have learned unconditional love and to do my best to demonstrate it in my life.

"I feel God has also given me a new opportunity to be a father with my daughter Sarah. She's been a pure blessing and a wonderful teacher to me of the power of love. She is teaching me all the time. She is a teacher of love, and now I am a very willing student. Before, I wasn't.

"My wife Christine has helped me make a difference. She's helped me change my life and has been a mirror for me. I believe that is what all relationships are for. Life is never really about the other person. We see something in other people and we say, 'I don't like that,' but it is really about us, about ourselves. Christine has reflected parts of me that I didn't like. They were showing up in her, and it bounced right back on me.

"It made me really take a hard look at who I was and how I was feeling about life and what my thoughts were. I began to see the love she gives me and I began to accept it. I know she loves me unconditionally. She has demonstrated that in so many ways. Before Christine, I didn't think I was worthy of love because I never had anyone love me in such a way."

Here Wally reminds us how our egos work and how easy it is to blame others and not to take responsibility for our thoughts and actions. I've seen how hard Wally works at reminding himself that everything he perceives is but a mirror of his own thoughts.

When we take responsibility for our own experiences and thoughts, the world looks different. Then, when we are in conflict, rather than taking the fruitless pathway of trying to change others, we can learn to change only our own thoughts and attitudes.

I next asked Wally to tell me how he got into the cookie business.

"I started baking chocolate chip cookies for friends back in 1970, like my Aunt Della had taught me to do. For five years I just gave them away. People had told me that they were so good that I should go into business and sell them. At the time, however, I was intent on being a big time show business manager. Then something different happened one night. A friend, B.J. Gilmore, said that she had a friend who could put up the money. She never found her friend, but I got some of my friends—Jeff Wall, Helen Reddy, and Marvin Gaye—and they put up the money and I put up everything else."

"Did you have any idea that it would take off like it did?"

"I knew it was a great idea," Wally said. "I knew it was going to be a success. I was going to open up one store on Sunset Boulevard just to make a living. At that time I had given up any desire to be famous. On March 10, 1975 we opened up the first store in the world that sold only chocolate chip cookies. It was a hit immediately."

And did Wally's cookie business ever grow! I have found sacks of his chocolate chip cookies with Wally's wonderful face staring out at me in hotels. And even in far-off places like Tokyo, I found his face on a very busy street in front of a Famous Amos Chocolate Chip Cookie store. It is difficult to find anyone who hasn't tasted his cookies. He put all of himself into that business, personally handling even the public relations for his company. It seemed that every time I turned on the TV, Wally was there advertising not only cookies but eggs, United Airlines, and long-distance telephone companies.

Today, Wally is no longer in the cookies business but he has a lot of irons in the fire, writing books, giving lectures, and he even has a wonderful television pilot that he is attempting to sell. He still does a lot of traveling, but his beautiful home remains in Hawaii just a few blocks from the beach.

Recently Wally was guided to write a purpose statement for himself. I found it very powerful and would like to share it with you.

My purpose for living is to be a servant of God, assisting Him in His work to help people realize their inner strength and greatness, to help them know they are not victims being manipulated by outside forces. To be a guide leading them to the God within, thereby having them discover their true power and nature, which is Love. I shall perform this assignment first and foremost by being a loving, positive example in all my thoughts, words, and deeds and by endeavoring at all times to be an open channel for God's guidance. My primary means of communicating God's message shall be writing books, recording audio and video cassettes, lecturing and appearing on television, and through motion pictures. I will also share with others any materials that might get them closer to God. I shall constantly listen for God's guidance as to whether I shall provide my services for a fee, or free of charge as I acknowledge that God is the source of all good in my life. Thank you, Father, for every opportunity to serve.

As we spoke about his life purpose, Wally went on to say, "There are a lot of things I want to do. I want to write more. I am very gratified that my new book, *The Power in You*, is getting so many wonderful responses from people whose lives are being improved, by changing their beliefs and changing their thinking.

"What are some of the things that you are most proud of?" I asked.

Wally's response: "I'm proud that the hat and the shirt from the original Famous Amos package is in the Smithsonian Institution. I'm proud of the Horatio Alger Award. Many people don't understand that it's really a group of guys and ladies who started with nothing and overcame tremendous obstacles and created meaningful lives for themselves. In 1987 I received that award, and every year we give college scholarships to students who might not otherwise go to college.

"For ten years I have been the national spokesperson for the Literacy Volunteers of America. I have spoken to millions of people and have given away tons of cookies to promote literacy. I've talked a lot about giving and I know that giving is the key. I'm on the board of directors of a group called Cities in Schools, and I've received much gratification from my participation in that wonderful organization."

I said, "I know that you've done much work in prisons. What advice would you give to someone who is in jail?"

Wally replied, "I see many people in prisons. I tell them that I see people who are holding inside themselves anger toward others and the people toward whom they feel the anger never really know this person is angry at them. So they go on living a very unfulfilled life, and the person who is holding on to this anger often winds up with disease, cancer or whatever. Also they never really know peace because every day of their lives they wake up with hatred and anger toward a person who isn't even aware of them in their daily life.

"I saw a great quote that said, 'Acid does more harm

to the vessel in which it is stored than to the object on which it is poured.' For me that is such a vivid image because that anger is an acid that eats your insides away. I ask people I visit in prison if they might be willing to find another way of looking at the world.

"I tell them that what works for me is like deciding not to have any more bummer thoughts. In effect, I'm saying to myself that I'm not going to have any more negative thoughts. I'm not going to depress myself or allow other people to depress me. I've come to the conclusion that thoughts are things. It takes a thought to produce anything. I have also stopped using the word *try*. I ask for guidance and I either do something or I don't. To me 'trying' means that maybe you will do something or maybe you won't. I want to make the commitment *to do*, not just to *try to do*. Loving and forgiving is what life is all about. It is something to do, not something to try to do.

"I want to have only good things in my life. So I work on having positive thoughts because I know my thoughts are going to be creating whatever happens in my world. When I visit people in prisons, I tell them that I do my best to experience everything that happens to me, no matter how catastrophic it may be, as a positive teaching that God would have me learn. That has really worked for me."

Here again we see in Wally a tremendous faith in God. Not a day goes by that he does not do the daily lesson from the Unity Church. What I appreciate about Wally is that his faith is unshakable. This comes across in his joy and exuberance for life. If there is anyone who shows a zest for living, it is Wally. He is a teacher of happiness and joy, and he reminds us that happiness is an internal matter and that when you have total faith in a loving Creative Force, nothing can interfere with that happiness.

71

I asked, "Wally, there will be some people reading this chapter who don't believe in God. Maybe their religious experiences were bad, or they feel that God is wrathful and punishing. What would you say to a person with that kind of belief system?"

"I'm not really trying to change other people or their beliefs. I think I'm more or less a door opener. I believe that whatever you believe is right for you. If, however, on any level your life isn't working, if there are parts of your life that you aren't comfortable with, if you really don't have peace of mind or don't know true joy and happiness, then I think you may want to re-examine your belief system."

I was aware that things had not always gone well in Wally's relationships with his three adult sons. However, today they are good friends and Wally's relationship with them is quite good. I asked him what it was that had made the difference.

Wally replied, "First of all, I had to learn to stop being attracted to guilt for all the mistakes I had made in the past. I had to really stop seeing value in guilt. And at the same time I had to learn to give it all to God. It was very clear to me that I was not able to do the job myself and needed all the help I could get. My last book, *The Power In You,* was actually written with my son Gregory, and the process of writing with him brought about even more healing.

"I feel God has also given me a new opportunity to be a father with my daughter, Sarah. She has been a pure blessing and a wonderful teacher to me on the power of love. She is teaching me all the time. She is a teacher of love, and now I am a very willing student. Before, I wasn't."

"What would you want engraved on your tombstone?" I asked Wally.

" 'Here's a happy, loving, and giving person who enjoyed life,' " he answered.

I am Wally's witness in saying that the way he lives his life is entirely consistent with that wish.

I told Wally that this was a book to remind people that we all make a difference, and asked him if there was anything he wanted to say about that.

He replied, "Everyone makes a difference whether we realize it or not. We are all role models. I believe that we need to know that even in the most menial jobs it is important to do our best. What do we want to pass on? What do we want our legacy to be? I think many people are really beginning to ask that question of themselves. We need to learn to believe one hundred percent in ourselves."

Afterword

Wally Amos has learned to walk very lightly on this earth. I have seen both him and Christine teach their daughter, Sarah, to love our planet by demonstration. They teach her to look, to see all the love that is in nature. And on their walks on the beach, they are joyfully and constantly picking up trash and litter that other people have left behind, expressing their love and respect and caring for our planet.

Wally is the epitome of the Good Humor Man. Every step he takes is a joyous one. Each day he seems to learn something new, something that he didn't know earlier in his life—that joy and happiness is our natural state.

One night I watched with amusement and delight as Wally led the Hawaiian Symphony Orchestra at a benefit, playing his kazoo and wearing a tuxedo jacket, bright Hawaiian shirt, black tie, and swimming trunks. I thought to myself that Wally Amos was one of the few people in the world who could get away with that.

Wally's loving energy is beyond effervescence and exuberance. When he comes into a room, it is like sunshine filling the whole space. And everyone simply feels great just being in his presence. There is no pretentiousness; there are no acts. It is just plain Wally, a beautiful child of God who has not forgotten his innocence or how to play and to be light. I have a lot of learning to do around the latter, because like so many others I am often tempted to take things too seriously.

Writer-artist and friend Joan Walsh Anglund, who has worked with Wally on *Literacy International*, says the following about Wally: "Wally is a man who truly believes, and because of his belief, he has an enormous amount of love energy to give to others."

Not long ago, author and friend Hugh Prather spoke at a fund-raising event for the Waldorf School in Santa Cruz, California. To a packed house at the Civic Auditorium, he introduced Wally as "God's court jester." I think that sums up Wally for me, whose playfulness offers so many valuable lessons for us all.

On March 18, 1990, there was an ABC Television Special in which President and Mrs. Bush presented the *President's National Literacy Awards*. That night, the Bushs presented Wally with the *National Literacy Award* for the countless hours he has devoted as the spokesman for "Literacy Volunteers of America."

Wally and his wife Christine continue each day to be wonderful teachers of giving and joy, sharing their unconditional love with everyone they meet.

4

LECH
WALESA

The awakened mind is one that knows
its source, its self, its holiness.

In Poland, which has known so much suffering since World War II, Lech Walesa's name and his dedication to easing the plight of his people shine through like a bright star. His is a determination that promises to keep shining forever.

The Polish people lived under martial law for two generations. They suffered from political oppression, economic depression, and the constant fear of punishment for speaking their own minds. Walesa's unshakable determination and faith in the dignity of his people has given hope and strength to all, helping the whole nation to seek a better way of life.

I wanted to interview Walesa because, of all the world figures I might have chosen, he best epitomizes how an ordinary man can achieve extraordinary things. For me his life seems to demonstrate beautifully that nothing is impossible when we have faith and we believe in something beyond ourselves, particularly in the ideals of true caring.

I picked him to interview not only because I admired him but because I wanted to meet him personally and to learn from him how he keeps the fire of passion alive in his heart in spite of so many setbacks. In January 1989, I read about a speech he gave in France, where he was being honored, in which he urged people to have a stronger belief in themselves and to have faith in an ideal greater than themselves. That article did it for me. In my meditation the next day, I experienced a feeling like a powerful magnet telling me that I had to meet Walesa, and that somehow the universe would arrange for me to do so.

As clear as this message was, my ego voice was equally insistent, telling me, "It is impossible to see Walesa. He is just too busy. Besides, you don't know anyone who knows him. It would just be a waste of time to try to see him."

Somehow, I managed to not listen to my ego voice that day. After asking for more guidance, I decided to send a cable to the head of the Time Magazine Bureau in Austria and ask for their help in getting me an appointment with Walesa.

To my surprise, I received a phone call giving me the name of a person in Warsaw who might help. I called that person and we talked on the phone for about an hour. He agreed to help me, and three days later he phoned back to say that I had been granted a two-hour appointment the following week. It was difficult for me to believe that it could be so easy, but it was.

A week after receiving this news, I flew to Poland, fortified with books about Walesa. In my reading I learned that he had come from a small rural village where no one could have predicted that he would someday be one of their country's most important leaders. I also learned that today Lech Walesa's name is a household word throughout his country and likely throughout the world. What has made him so well known is his leadership in the Solidarity Movement, a labor organization fighting for workers' rights and an end to poverty.

As a very young man, Walesa had no ambition to become involved in political issues. Then, after finishing his primary education, he studied for an apprenticeship as an electrician and was assigned to work in the shipyards at Gdańsk. He quickly saw that working conditions there were horrendous, the pay was very poor, safety standards were dismal, and there was a great feeling of depression and helplessness among the workers. The trade union, now known as Solidarity, was formed and it began to make demands on the government for better pay and safer working conditions.

Many Solidarity supporters were found murdered. Despite this, an amazingly determined force of minds came together. They shared a common belief in freedom, dignity, and respect for all. They were not going to allow themselves to be dominated by fear. Under Walesa's leadership they also came to realize that the ideals they were fighting for could be reached through peaceful means.

Throughout the long years of Solidarity's struggle, not everyone has agreed with Walesa. But most have felt that he offered a new way, where people could play a part in shaping their own destiny. At a time when so many people could find little to respect in their government and were losing hope in their future and themselves, it was clear that Walesa was one man who believed that nothing is impossible, that you truly can make a difference when you believe in yourself.

For many years the government of Poland made Solidarity illegal, and Walesa was marked as a rebel. Although Walesa's life was threatened many times, he stood his ground, totally committed to his ideals. He continued to work day and night for better working conditions and wages for the workers in the shipyards, and for better economic conditions for everyone.

Walesa was arrested and sent to prison many times.

Although he suffered great hardships in prison, his influence throughout the country increased. He was absolutely dedicated to helping his people have freedom of speech and to have a voice in government. Although the government refused to meet with Walesa, Solidarity grew. Then, in 1983, the whole world learned of Walesa and his country's struggle when he was awarded the Nobel Peace Prize.

Turning Points

Even as I was flying to Poland, there were dramatic new changes being announced in that country. In a surprise move, the government made an offer to legalize Solidarity if Walesa could promise them that there would not be a workers' strike for two years. This was a momentous occasion in Poland's history. In a country that had known so much hardship and had struggled so long with feelings of hopelessness, the government's surprising offer was one of the brightest rays of hope the Polish people had experienced for many decades.

Upon my arrival in Warsaw, my newfound friend, who had arranged my appointment with Walesa, met me at the airport. After we got into his car, we shared the good news about the government's change of heart and he told me that the talk in the streets was that Walesa was already being urged to become the next prime minister. Then came the bad news: he had just received word from Walesa's secretary that my interview had been canceled. Due to the recent developments, Walesa was too busy to meet with me.

Although I felt exhilarated by the news that the government was going to recognize Solidarity, I was more than deeply disappointed that our interview had been called off. To tell you the truth, I felt absolutely devastated. As we drove to my hotel, I asked myself why I had come all this way, halfway around the world. Was it just a wasted trip?

I even considered turning around and taking the next plane home. But I decided against it. I checked into my hotel and that night decided to pray for guidance. When I awoke the next morning, after a restless night, I began to feel a sense of peace within myself and some clarity about what I should do.

I had read in a book about Walesa that one of his closest friends was Father Jankowsky, who had a church in Gdańsk, where Walesa lived. Father Jankowsky had been an active supporter of Solidarity for years and, like Walesa, his life had been threatened for his beliefs. In many ways Father Jankowsky and Walesa were like devoted brothers, and they spent much time together.

My guidance was that I should somehow meet with Father Jankowsky and he would help me get my interview with Walesa. I tried phoning Father Jankowsky several times but all the phone circuits to Gdańsk were busy. I finally decided to rent a taxi and drive to Gdańsk, over four hours away. A friend of a friend who lived in Warsaw agreed to come along and act as my interpreter.

As we drove out of Warsaw, the sky was gray and overcast. I became aware of how extremely flat the country was here. The faces of the people I saw on the streets seemed mostly somber and depressed. Most store windows were empty or had very little in them. Then, as we left the outskirts of the city, the rural countryside became quite pretty. For a while I felt as if I had been projected back in time. In the farming areas, the equipment I saw was ancient, belonging to a previous century. There were many small carts pulled by horses or mules.

We stopped in a small restaurant for lunch. There, I got another picture of the kinds of difficulties people faced in a country that was suffering so much economic hardship. Things we take so much for granted in the United States were difficult in Poland. For example, at the restaurant I discovered that there was a toilet paper shortage. There was half a roll of toilet paper sitting beside the cash register. The paper was sold by the foot to customers who wished to use the bathrooms downstairs.

The general feeling I had during my week in Poland was one of heaviness, superimposed on feelings of helplessness. Although everyone I met was quite friendly to me, there were not many happy faces. People had gone without for such a very long time that it had become difficult for them to believe that the future could be any different.

We finally arrived in Gdańsk. It was much larger than I had imagined and was a very busy city. We found the church and rectory of Father Jankowsky on the outskirts of the city. The church reminded me of many churches that I had seen in towns throughout the United States. In the church itself there were several meeting rooms and the whole place was bustling with activity. Next door to the church was the rectory, where Father Jankowsky lived. Through my interpreter I discovered that Father Jankowsky was not there at the moment but was expected to return in about fifteen minutes.

There were several people ahead of me waiting to see Father Jankowsky. After about forty-five minutes, he came out into the waiting room, greeted me, and took me into his study. He was a large-framed man with, I was glad to see, a very friendly face.

I quickly learned that he didn't speak a word of English, so my interpreter was kept very busy. I told

Father Jankowsky about the book I was writing, explaining that I wanted it to inspire readers to know that each of us really does make a difference. I went on to explain how disappointed I was not to be able to interview Lech Walesa, as we'd planned. I told him that I wanted to learn more about Walesa's spiritual beliefs and that I was not a reporter here to question him about his politics.

I then asked Father Jankowsky if he could share with me a little about himself and his relationship with Walesa. I wanted him to give me his impressions of Walesa the man, since these two men had known each other for many years. Father Jankowsky told me that the God spirit had always been within Walesa and that his faith has contributed much to his ability to trust his intuition for making the right decisions. He said that Walesa feels a special calling to work for God, to help the people of Poland gain dignity and take control of their lives and to make life better for everyone.

Father Jankowsky told me that Walesa has eight children ranging from the ages of three to eighteen years. He told me that in his heart Walesa is very much a family man, and that it pains him that his work keeps him away from his family so much. When I asked Father Jankowsky which single trait impressed him the most about Walesa, he replied, "It is his steadfastness and his commitment to God. He has a God spirit and a strong intuition for making the right choices and decisions, following God's directions. He totally believes in his ideals and he doesn't allow any doubts to enter."

Father Jankowsky then interrupted our interview to make a phone call. I didn't realize that he was calling Walesa's secretary and asking him to come over to meet with me. A few minutes after the call, a man about thirty-five years old joined us, but he was not introduced to me until later. It turned out that he was Walesa's secretary and that they both were checking me out.

Father Jankowsky asked me a number of questions about my work. He seemed particularly interested in the work we do at our Center for Attitudinal Healing, where we work with children who are experiencing catastrophic illness. About an hour and a half later, Father Jankowsky and Walesa's secretary went into the corner of the room and conferred in Polish.

In a few minutes they came back with smiles on their faces and informed me that if I returned at six that evening I could have my interview with Walesa in Father Jankowsky's study. Walesa's secretary went on to say, to my great surprise and delight, that I would have an appointment with Walesa's wife and children the next day at their home. I was absolutely thrilled about this because I knew that Mrs. Walesa rarely gave interviews.

I was also given the address of Walesa's older sister who lived in another city. She had no phone but they said they felt sure that she would be willing to see me. It was a little hard for me to believe my good fortune. I left with my interpreter and we drove around the city, saw the huge shipyards, visited some monuments, and then had tea.

Although I would not see Walesa's sister Isabella until the following day, I think that it might be interesting to share a few of her comments now, since they give us a view of her brother that the media rarely touches. First I'd like to say that Isabella is a middle-aged, cheerful woman who could not have been more open, friendly, and cooperative. She told me that in his school days her brother Lech had been just an average kid who worked hard at his assignments and chores. He hadn't really excelled in anything specific, except that he did have a natural talent for working with mechanical things. He had never had any dreams of doing anything unusual in his life and certainly had never dreamed that he might one day be famous.

Isabella told me that Lech was always helping out his family and other people. He always seemed to have a sense of caring for others. She said that when he first went to work in the shipyards he was a chain smoker, and people saw him as an angry young man. She said he felt incensed by the injustices at work, the poor pay, the terrible working conditions, the lack of food, and the many other difficulties that he and his fellow workers encountered.

I asked if she could remember any humorous events from the past, and she told me of an experience that had happened when Lech was about eighteen years old. "It was one of the two times that I know of him getting drunk," she said. "My other brother was also so drunk that day that he could not walk home. So Lech tried to carry him home on his back, holding on to only his coat. When Lech finally made it to our front door, I asked him where our brother was. And Lech replied, 'Why, he is right here on my back.' " Isabella then pointed out to Lech that he was holding onto their brother's empty coat. Lech immediately looked around and discovered, to his amazement, that his brother indeed was not there. He turned around and stumbled back down the hill in search of him.

Going back to the events of January 25, we arrived at Father Jankowsky's at about a quarter to six. Our taxi driver became quite excited because he recognized Walesa's white van parked in front of the rectory.

Upon entering the church, we were immediately ushered into Father Jankowsky's study, and within seconds Mr. Walesa came in. The room seemed to fill to overflowing with the energy of his charisma. He wore a blue suit, had a broad smile on his face, and his eyes flashed with excitement. As we started the interview, I felt he really didn't understand what it was to be about and that he had agreed to talk with me only because Father Jankowsky had suggested it.

His physical appearance was somewhat different than I had expected. He had put on weight and had a bigger potbelly than I remembered from the pictures I'd seen. The long hair that I had seen in newspaper photos was now much shorter, and his bushy mustache had been trimmed.

He talked rather quickly, in a staccato fashion, and his eyes sparkled with energy as we conversed. He was charming, quick-witted, and very animated, and his body was always in motion.

I explained to Walesa, "In this interview with you, I'm not primarily interested in your politics. What really interests me is finding out what is inside you that has helped you to make a difference in your country and in the world. Would you share with me a little about your spiritual beliefs?"

With much feeling and sincerity Walesa replied, "Without my trust and faith in God I would have no hope. My faith in God has been the source of my courage."

These words went straight to my heart. I believe that is why the people who come to our Center in Tiburon seem to have such peace. Even though they are facing perhaps the most difficult challenges of their lives, they have a belief in something beyond themselves.

They seem to find a peace of mind, a peace of God, through their willingness to help one another. They are no longer fixed on only those things that might benefit themselves. They have let go and let God run the show and be the director of their lives. And this is what Walesa was saying—that nothing is impossible when you have total trust and faith in God.

"Prayer is essential in my life," Walesa continued. "I believe that each of us, to be fully alive, must have a belief in something beyond ourselves." After a brief pause and almost with tears in his eyes, he added, "I would also like to say that the love and support of my wife and Father Jankowsky has been critcally important to me."

I asked him if he could tell me the source of his beliefs. Had someone taught him these things or had he come to them by himself?

He answered, "The things that I have fought for and held close to my heart were really things that my mother taught me. There were values such as honesty, integrity, fair play, equality, and justice."

As he spoke, it was very clear to me that these were no idle words for him. This was a man who did his best to live by the principles in which he believed. One of the things that impressed me about him was his deep sense of the importance of equality for all people. Even though he was now a world figure and had helped inspire thousands of people to work for a better life, he did not put himself above others. He stated his feelings about this in a very simple but wonderfully eloquent way:

"You can't help others unless you are one of them and you treat them as equals. For example, I feel it is most important that I continue to work with the people on the job. My day starts at five in the morning. I work at the shipyards as an electrician until two in the afternoon. I then go to the Solidarity office and often work late into the night." Then, half-jokingly, he added, "My secretary at the Solidarity office comes to work at ten A.M., works much shorter hours, and gets far better pay than I."

As we spoke, I got the impression that Walesa had no particular heroes or role models. He was his own man, doing his best to listen to his own inner guidance. He had a strong sense of justice, fairness, and personal integrity. And he believed with all his heart that there could eventually be openness and equality in his country.

Over and over again in the interview Walesa stressed that we are not here to judge one another but to find better ways of communicating with one another. As to finding solutions, Walesa said, "We have no choice but to find peaceful solutions. It is not a feeling of obligation but it is a deep-seated feeling I have that it is only through prayer and discussion based on prayer that we can find peace."

Through his life his faith in God has given him hope and has allowed him to believe that nothing is impossible. He felt certain that as long as he had his faith and his hope, the future was going to be better and that nobody had to be limited by the past.

Walesa spoke much about the Solidarity movement. His experiences had convinced him more than ever that solutions to even the largest social problems can be found through open dialogue—and without violence. In the early strikes in his country many workers had been killed, and as we talked about it I could tell that these terrible sacrifices weighed very heavily on his heart.

As I thought about his struggles, I had to admire the depth of his faith. He had worked hard and long at solving the problems of his country in a peaceful way, and he had never given up. He had faced many frustrations, many actions by other people that some would have felt were unforgivable, worthy of deep anger. I asked Walesa, "How do you handle your anger?"

His rapidfire speech slowed as he answered, "In the past few years I think I have learned to deal with my anger much better. I now have faith that with open dialogue and optimism we can always find alternatives to condemning or attacking each other." He added, "There are many people who say very negative things about me and who sometimes attack me for my beliefs. But I am no longer bothered by other people's judgments of me."

During our conversation, a man entered the room, tapped Walesa on the shoulder, and whispered something in his ear. Walesa then asked me to follow him. We entered a rather large bathroom. Without saying a word, Walesa proceeded to remove his coat, tie, shirt, and undershirt and sat on a chair in front of a mirror. I couldn't even imagine what was happening. At that moment another man came into the room and draped a white sheet around Walesa.

Walesa looked up at me and laughed. "I am about to get a haircut. I'll bet you have never conducted an interview while someone was getting a haircut."

"No," I admitted. "This is a first for me. I think God must have a wonderful sense of humor to put us together in this bathroom on the eve of such a momentous time in the history of your people, a day before you will be meeting with the government."

We both laughed, and when Walesa laughed he did so with his whole body.

Our talk then turned to his family, which is very important to him. He said that he loves spending time at home with his children, playing with them and praying with them at night. He enjoys helping them with their schoolwork, and he deeply regrets that he doesn't have more time to spend with them.

Working long hours and being a leader were not the things that he most desired, he said. Rather, he would much prefer to go fishing or to go hunting for wild mushrooms with his family.

"Obviously, " he said, "God has other plans for me. I

do not always like the things I do, but God tells me to do them, and so I do. It is difficult for me to be a public person. I would much rather have a quieter life. There is never enough time to do all the things I feel I need to do, and I always feel under pressure, always rushing.

"I do believe that I am one of those whom God has appointed to awaken the Polish people to their own dignity, their own ability to stand up and be accounted for, to claim freedom of speech, to express our own thoughts, and to vote and not be afraid. I believe that these are the natural gifts that God gives to us and that each of us must learn to claim.

"Although I have a deep belief in God, I don't believe in telling other people what to believe. I am no saint. I'm human and I commit my share of sins and make my share of mistakes. When the time comes for me to leave this planet, I am not at all sure that I won't end up in hell."

"If after you are dead and gone you could have only one sentence on your tomb, what would you want it to say?" I asked.

He quickly replied, "No one has ever asked me that question before." After a moment's careful thought, he went on, "I am a simple man. I cannot think of anything I would want it to say. I wouldn't want a monument or flowers. A prayer for me and the sign of the cross and for people to hold me in their hearts would be all I would need."

After this, we discussed his marriage. He told me that he and his wife don't always agree on everything; sometimes they argue, but their arguments are short-lived. He said that when officers came to arrest him his wife was pregnant, soon to give birth.

He was very proud of the role she had played in going to Sweden to receive his Nobel Peace Prize. At the time, he felt that he was needed in Poland and that it would not be wise for him to take the time to leave. After much prayer, he decided that his wife should receive the prize on his behalf. He felt that she deserved to be there because of all the sacrifices and the hard work she had done for Solidarity. He was very proud that everyone liked her and of the wonderful job she did in representing him and the Polish people.

The next day, when I spoke with his wife at their home, I found her to be a very humble woman. I also had the opportunity of meeting the Walesas' three youngest daughters, who were playing outside. The children were very charming and I took photographs of them. Later, back in the States, I was pleased to find that the pictures had come out well, and I sent the Walesas copies of them.

One of the questions I asked Mrs. Walesa that day had to do with the difficulties and hardships her family had suffered over the past twenty years. I was surprised by her answer: "We have been married for nineteen years, and I do not think it was an extremely hard life. Everybody has troubles and so it is just a normal life." She admitted that when her husband was jailed her life was very difficult and that she had gotten very angry at the time because she was pregnant with their youngest child.

I asked her if there was anything she would change about her husband. She answered that she would not change him because then he would not be Lech. Then, perhaps as an afterthought, she added, "He is too fat. I want him to be more slim."

Since her dedication to her family was so very important to her, I asked what traits she would like her children to develop. In her answer she expressed many of those same beliefs and feelings that her and her husband's lives so strongly expressed: "I want them to develop steadfastness, an appreciation for the importance of acting on your convictions. Everyone should act with conviction in what he is doing."

She spoke of the time when her husband was jailed and she became a connection between him and the outside world. This became the main task in her life during that period, and, added to the responsibilities to her huge family, it could not have been easy for her.

As she told me these things about their family life, I suddenly had a clearer picture of the kind of close and caring relationship they shared. Both husband and wife had faith in a force larger than themselves, combined with a deep caring for their own family and for their country and its people.

In the last part of my interview with Lech Walesa, I told him I had heard that the people of Poland wanted him to be their prime minister. I asked, "What would you do if you heard God telling you, sometime in the future, to get out of the private sector and become the prime minister?"

He replied quite thoughtfully and seriously, "If that happened, I would think that God must be very angry with me because God knows that I don't want to become a politician." After a few moments of silence, and with a smile on his face, he added, "Indeed, I would do what God asked me to do, but God has not asked me that yet."

Afterword

As I write this many things have happened in Poland that even a year ago no one would have dreamed possible. Solidarity has been recognized by the government, Walesa and his colleages are meeting at intervals with government officials, and there have been free elections with many Solidarity candidates being elected.

Lech Walesa was asked to run for prime minister of Poland, but he declined, saying that he could better serve his people in other ways. Instead, another of the Solidarity leaders is running for that office. The beginning of a democratic process is taking place in a peaceful manner. And Walesa has journeyed to Italy once again to meet the Pope.

Walesa's popularity is now greater than ever. Other countries, including the United States, are now coming forth with financial aid to Poland. There are still many economic problems. There are those who feel that Walesa's ways are too slow; they still wish to strike.

Walesa and the Polish people continue to face many challanges. Having met Walesa, I know one thing for sure: he will never stop putting all the effort of his very being into bringing dignity, self-respect, and a better way of life to all the people of Poland. Behind this man's strength is his belief in himself and the conviction that nothing is impossible. But even beyond these is an almost unbelievable strength that comes from his belief, trust, and faith in God.

After hearing him tell his story, I saw that there had been many situations during his lifetime when he hadn't known which way to turn, but prayer continued to give him strength and courage. He knew that he was not alone. He also knew that God's way was a peaceful one. Walesa taught me much that day about being clearly focused, without any doubts about trusting God's wisdom and direction.

Walesa was not a "sort of" person, as so many of us can be. He doesn't "sort of" put his efforts in one direction . . . and then if he discovers bumps in the road gets frustrated and quits. What got to me, and what I hope gets to you, was his total commitment to an ideal beyond himself.

Walesa seems to be well aware of his ego desires,

and there is part of him that could have worked in the shipyards and spent most of his spare time fishing and hunting wild mushrooms. In many ways he could see that this way of life would have been easier. But it was clear to him that this wasn't what God wanted him to do. Somehow he knew that he could only be happy doing his best to let God's will and his will be one. I also respected that he made no efforts to push his religious beliefs on to other people.

To me, Lech Walesa is a beautiful example of how one ordinary man can accomplish extraordinary things and truly make a difference. He has an inner knowing that when your faith and trust in God is total, and when prayer plays an essential role in your life, peace and clarity come into your thinking.

For me, perhaps one of the most important things he said was to remind me that we are not here to judge one another, but to love and care for one another. It seems to me that this is at the very core of his thinking, helping to bring together the people of his country and the government, to find peaceful and loving solutions to the many hardships that they have faced and to those that lie ahead for them.

Walesa demonstrates for all of us that each of us really can make a difference. We can each help bring about social change, justice, fairness, and a belief in human equality when we commit all of ourselves to an ideal with the common denominator of communicating with honesty, nonviolence, and true caring.

1990

So much has happened since my interview with Lech Walesa in January 1989! Primarily due to his efforts, a whole new democratic process has been given life in Poland. Among other changes, the country is now being led by a member of the Solidarity Party.

The triumph of the "ordinary people's will" has brought about miraculous changes in everyday life and in the political structure of Eastern Europe. Many people have attributed these changes to what happened in Poland under Lech Walesa's leadership.

Since my meeting with him, Mr. Walesa has visited the United States and has addressed a Joint Session of Congress. Wherever he appeared in his travels to this country, he received a hero's welcome.

Perhaps as much as any person alive, Lech Walesa has proven to us all how much power to change the world the ordinary person can have when that person is in partnership with the Supreme Being. Mr. Walesa has shown the world that when you're committed to helping others—and you persevere steadfastly—miracles really do occur. He teaches us that ideals of fairness, trust and love can and do win out, making this a better world for us all.

.

CHAPTER

5

RUTH
BRINKER

Giving and receiving are the same.

Whenever people tell me that they would like to find a way to do something helpful and meaningful in the world, I immediately think of Ruth Brinker, who found her way to be helpful by tuning into the needs of the people around her in her everyday life. She is a wonderful reminder to me, and to all of us, that perhaps the first step toward being helpful to others is to slow down, to look beyond ourselves and to give our full attention to what is going on around us.

As I spoke with Ruth Brinker, I was moved by her commitment to make it a personal priority to be helpful to others. The question, "What can I do to be helpful?" seems constantly in her mind. The more I learned about her, the more I was convinced that our world would undergo dramatic healing if all of us could sincerely have that question in our minds in all our relationships: "What can I do to be helpful?" She teaches us that to make a difference in the world, we have only to open our hearts to see a need and then to go forward with the resolve never to be discouraged by what appear to be obstacles.

Ruth is the founder and director of a San Francisco project called Open Hands, which helps to feed AIDS patients who are too ill to leave their homes. One of the first questions I asked Ruth was, "What motivated you to start Open Hands? How did it get started?"

She replied, "It was back in 1984. A young friend who was an architect became ill with AIDS. I was appalled at how quickly his illness progressed. He lost weight and went downhill so rapidly that soon he was too ill to take care of himself. Some friends and I formed a rotating caretaker group and would drop in on him to visit and to bring meals. Occasionally someone would forget about his or her shift and our dying friend would go hungry until the next shift.

"I realized then that there had to be many people throughout the city who did not have a support system like my friend's. And I recognized that the number of AIDS patients was only going to increase. I felt that many people with AIDS were really dying of malnutrition, not AIDS, because many of them didn't have the energy to go to the grocery store and no one was available to bring them food. I suddenly realized that there was no way for most people with AIDS to get meals. So I started Open Hands.

"I had been running Meals on Wheels out of Trinity Church, so I started serving people with AIDS from the same location. With one hand I was doing Meals on Wheels and with the other I was cooking and packaging meals for people with AIDS, which I delivered myself. I started with just seven people, whose names I had gotten from the AIDS Foundation.

"I had anticipated starting with many more, but that was all the names I got. I had the feeling that people didn't take me seriously. They thought I was some silly *hausfrau* that had a nice idea, but that it would never come to fruition."

"You started very slowly, then," I said. "What kind of help did you have at that time?"

"Initially, there was just me. Then very slowly I began to gather volunteers. By the end of 1986 we were serving a hundred people, two meals per day for each person. We served a hot dinner entrée and a bag lunch for the following day. Our volunteers would pick up the lunches and deliver them right to the AIDS patients' homes.

"From the very beginning I was determined to provide only very good food. We've never used anything but fresh vegetables and never any processed food of any kind. And the bread we use was always a Tassajara bread, which people in this area know as excellent whole-grain bread. At first I wanted to serve fancy foods, but I quickly learned that when you are ill you want simple food—the kinds of food that mother used to make. So I switched over to pot roasts, meatloaf, mashed potatoes, and that kind of thing."

"It seems to me that Open Hands has grown very quickly," I said. "It's become a model for similar programs all around the country. Could you tell us a little about how that has happened?"

"We received a great deal of favorable publicity in 1987 and 1988. I received KRON Television's For Those Who Care Award. I also received the Dorothy Langson Humanitarian Award. Every time I received publicity for an award it would result in contributions from the general public, and our client list would then grow some more. So by the beginning of 1988 we were serving 350 people, 700 meals a day, and now in 1989 we are serving over 500 people, 1,000 meals per day, and we have over 400 volunteers who deliver the food in their own cars."

I remarked, "I understand that you outgrew your old kitchen and have a new one now."

"That's right. We now have a new kitchen at the foot of Potrero Hill, at 2720 17th Street. And from a kitchen of about 500 square feet we now have one that's almost 4,000 square feet. It's really a state-of-the-art kitchen with the very best equipment."

"That is a very rapid growth!" I said. "How did you get the finances to increase the number of meals you were serving and to open the new kitchen?"

Ruth thought for a moment, then replied: "I really believe in miracles, and I know I'm not doing this alone, that God is always there to help take away obstacles. Initially we received two thouand dollars from the Zen Center and another two thousand from the Golden Gate Business Association.

"I found that I really didn't know anything about writing up grants for foundations. KRON Television had made a four-minute videotape telling of our program at Open Hands and of my receiving their award. After the awards dinner, the producer gave me a copy of the tape, and the next day I went to the Chevron Corporation with it. The miracle was that without my writing a formal grant proposal, eight days later they gave us a $125,000 grant."

"What is your yearly budget now?" I asked.

"Our budget is $3.2 million. Most of it goes for direct services, like food, packaging, and salaries for the kitchen staff. And as we look ahead to 1990, we see a need to expand our services to the I.V. drug-using population of the area. By 1990, we will probably be serving twelve hundred people, over twenty-four hundred meals per day."

"How are you going to reach the drug users?" I asked, knowing that this problem is increasing at such a rapid pace today.

Ruth replied, "We're going to use clinics such as the Haight-Ashbury Clinic, which deals primarily with substance-abuse problems, and Glide Memorial Church. Cecil Williams [the director and pastor of Glide] and his church do remarkable work helping people who are using hard drugs, and when they are too ill to come to the church to get a meal, we step in and deliver meals to them."

"It seems to me," I said, "that this kind of program is needed everywhere in the world, in every major city where we see so many of these same problems. Do you have any plans to train other people in different parts of the United States to do what you are doing?"

"We already are," Ruth replied. "The Woods Johnson Foundation gave us a grant to produce a step-by-step training manual, and also an institutional cookbook. We have already helped in starting an Open Hands in Chicago and in Atlanta. We also assisted a group in New York City called God's Love, We Deliver. And then there's a group in Dallas called Meals on the Move, and the acronym is MOM. So, whenever anyone with AIDS is hungry and needs a meal, they call MOM."

"How long do you think you will be doing this?" I asked.

Ruth's response was quick and enthusiastic: "I will be doing it forever. I don't foresee retirement at all. I just thrive on what I'm doing. It excites me, stimulates me, and energizes me. I'm also excited about a new cookbook being published by Simon and Schuster. Fifty-two celebrity chefs were asked to write their favorite menus for preparing a meal for their closest and most loved friends. It was the idea of Robert Schneider, who is a chef. The royalties are going to Open Hands, and we are most delighted and appreciative that you, Jerry, wrote the foreword for that book.

"There is one thing I would like to add, and that is that we are hoping to raise money by offering food services for Child Daycare Centers. We will charge a fee and drop the meals off at the daycare centers so that when parents come by to pick up their children in the evening, they can also pick up meals. This will help them spend some quality time with their children rather than spending that time after work shopping and preparing meals and cleaning up afterward."

As Ruth shared the story of Open Hands with me, I began to reflect on how creative she has allowed her mind to be. She does not depend on the government for any of the financing of Open Hands. She clearly knows that when there is a will to be truly helpful and loving to others, there is a Creative Love Force in the universe that will help us find a way. What a beautiful and original way it is to be of service both to working parents and to AIDS patients. Ruth is a wonderful teacher, demonstrating that when your vision is clear and you continue to believe in it, obstacles will be removed and a way will be revealed for you to fulfill your vision of love.

I wanted to know more about what was behind a person like this, who would dedicate herself to making such a difference in her community. I asked, "What motivates a person to do what you're doing?"

"I had a deep inner need to do it," she replied. "I had a vision of people all over San Francisco who were too weak to take care of themselves. I also had visions of my friend who died of AIDS, multiplied hundreds of times over, and I felt that I needed to do something about it.

"For as long as I can remember, I've felt that if someone who was in trouble crossed my path I had an obligation to help them as much as I could."

As I thought about her answer, I remembered many of the famous people who had similar visions of life down through the years, and I wondered if Ruth had been influenced by any of them. I asked, "Did you have any particular role models in your life, people who were your teachers or whose lives influenced yours?"

Ruth said, "I have always loved to read Tolstoy. Gandhi actually got his principles of nonviolence from Tolstoy. In my way of looking at it, Tolstoy excerpted everything that Christ said in the Bible and came up with a simple philosophy of love.

"Another person who influenced me in an important way was Aldous Huxley's teacher, Swami Prabhavanada of the Vedanta Society in Southern California. I was brought up in the midwest, where if you were not in the Judeo-Christian classification it is believed that you must be involved in superstition. Therefore, anything from the Far East was relegated to paganism and superstition and was not to be given any credibility at all. So I thought it was very curious that someone as brilliant as Aldous Huxley should be influenced by the man from India.

"I decided that the next time I was in Southern California I would try to meet this man, Swami Prabhavanada. I was never so impressed by anyone in my life! He spoke so simply and he quoted the Bible. His interpretations of portions of the Bible seemed to make much more sense than ones I had previously heard."

"I know it is often difficult to put spiritual experiences into words," I said, "but could you tell us a little more about how this experience changed your life?"

"It's going to sound strange," Ruth said. "I only heard him speak two or three times, but at one point he said that anyone could experience God in about three minutes. Anyone could have a mystical experience. And he said that if we would simply quiet our minds, wipe all thoughts from our minds, we would feel *something* and that *something* would be the beginning of a relationship with God. So, I did it.

"It was much more difficult than I'd thought it would be. But I found that by concentrating very intensely I was able to do it. I was in my apartment and I took my phone off the hook and buried it under the pillows. I was flooded with this wonderful calm and loving euphoria. I was young then and very busy, so when I put the phone back on the hook, it rang. I had a lot of distractions, and in those days I turned to God only when I was deeply troubled.

"Then one day I had a problem and I was sobbing on my bed. I suddenly realized that I was involved in self-pity and decided to quiet my mind and go into a meditative state. I was immediately filled with a wonderful calm and euphoria, and it was at that point that I began practicing it on a regular basis. And I have never experienced that kind of unhappiness again."

"Are you thinking about God as you talk to me now?"

"Yes," Ruth replied. "I guess there's a part of my mind that keeps calm and euphoric while I go about doing whatever needs to be done. I have this connection to God all the time. I have no religious preference. The director of Trinity Episcopal, where Open Hands started, likes to see me in the congregation occasionally. And so I sometimes go there as a courtesy to him. I also have friends who are Catholic, and I go to their churches too. But it is not because I'm drawn to either one or the other."

"What about any other people who have influenced you?" I asked.

"I have been very much influenced by Lao Tzu, who wrote a small book titled *Tao Te Ching* that was translated by Stephen Mitchell. He has written this wonderful, simple philosophy, a way of life that embodies most of what I have learned through my own meditation."

Next I asked, "Could you share a little about your

very early life, such as where were you born and what it was like for you when you were growing up?"

"I was born in South Dakota in 1922. My father was a wheat farmer and was always interested in science. He had a great love of nature, horses, and dogs. Unfortunately, we never had much of a relationship with each other until he was dying. He was very detached from my older brother and me and would easily become outraged. But when he was dying I really began to love him a great deal more than I ever had before."

"What about your mother?" I asked.

"I didn't have a very good relationship with her either. She brought me up to be afraid of my father, and when I was a very small child she made me promise never to marry. There was much I had to learn to forgive her for, but I believe that I have forgiven her completely now. In growing up I saw her as pretty superficial and self-centered. I really didn't like her much, but my brother and I were very close."

"Is your mother living?"

"No, she died a few years ago," Ruth replied.

"What about your early adult life?" I asked. "Could you tell us something about that?"

"I worked as a model in San Francisco and then I married Jack Brinker, a designer, in 1955. We have two daughters, Lisa, thirty-two years old, and Sara, thirty-one. Jack died of cancer in 1970. To be honest, I have to say that our marriage had a lot of conflict and disharmony in it and many, many challenges. I had an antique shop and finances were difficult. I also wrote a dog column for the *San Francisco Examiner*."

"Can we go back to your project Open Hands for a moment? Many people have started projects as you did, but after confronting a few obstacles they quit. Certainly you have faced and overcome hundreds of obstacles along the way, but you have persevered.

What do you think it is that has allowed you to go on when you were faced with one hurdle after another?"

She had an interesting response: "Jerry, I think I have an inner tenacity and stubbornness, that this is what God wants me to do and it will be done. I do feel that I'm doing what God wants me to do or I wouldn't be having all these miracles occurring at just the right time. I have always known that I am just an instrument. I never could do it by myself, without God."

"Ruth, I would like you to imagine that you are in a grammar school today talking to fifth- and sixth-graders, giving them suggestions or advice on how to make a difference. What would you tell them?"

"I would really have to give that a lot of thought. I think I would give some kind of message about love. I believe that teaching occurs without speaking. I know that is what I try to do—I try to live by example. And so I would try to give some kind of message urging young people to love."

Afterword

I find it frustrating to try to find exactly the right words to describe other people, to capture their essence with words. But I'll attempt to do this by saying that there is a light that reflects from Ruth's eyes, and that the essence of her being lights up the room. There is a sense of quietude and peace that is most contagious. One does not have to hear Ruth's words to be able to feel her peace and her love. Being with her is like being covered with a blanket of love.

I was most impressed by her complete commitment to do what she perceives as God's work and her belief that nothing is impossible. Ruth makes it clear that it is not so much your profession or social status in life that counts, but what you do to make this world a better place. She is so very clear about her connection to God and that she is but an instrument. It is her simplicity that is most endearing to me, reminding me that the way of loving, giving, and happiness is not complicated but very simple indeed. All it takes is complete trust and faith.

Ruth's life, in every action and word, seems an embodiment of this trust and faith. It is a trust and faith that allows her to slow down, to look beyond herself and really give her full attention to help the people in the world around her.

CHAPTER

6

TED
TURNER

Do not forget that your will has power
Over all fantasies and dreams.
Trust it to see you through,
And carry you beyond them.

For a long time I have believed that each of us has many facets to his personality. The personality is much like a house with a thousand windows. And what others see in us may seem to change, depending on which of our windows they choose to look through. When I think about this, I cannot help but reflect on how frequently I have myself judged another person's entire personality by only a single window. One of the many lessons Ted Turner has taught me is not to be distracted by the negative aspects of others' personalities but to choose to see more clearly the positive ones.

When you are a famous person like Ted Turner, people who don't know you well tend to fix their attention on the personality facets that are highlighted in the media. We ignore all the other parts, though there may be hundreds of them.

Rather than being manipulated by what the media says, or by what other people might say, we can actually choose which parts of the personality we wish to see. We need not limit ourselves to the view provided through a single window.

Before I met Ted Turner, I had read and had heard an assortment of stories about him. What had impressed me most were the stories about his commitment to the environment and to peace, and the many different ways he was making real contributions to better these causes. What impressed me the least were the stories that depicted him as a man who walked all over other people, who was insensitive to others' feelings, who was overly absorbed in himself, and who would figuratively eat people up with his anger. I must admit that I had made many judgments about him based on these stories.

I think that very few people who have ever met Ted Turner come away with neutral feelings about him. They like and admire him, or they despise him. There just doesn't seem to be any gray area where opinions about this man are concerned. In some people's eyes, he is a Don Juan type. Others claim he is a person with a temper that is hard to control. To others, he seems to be a person who is anything but easy to be relaxed and peaceful around; the force of his energy seems to raise storms of confusion or controversy wherever he goes. This last characteristic was one that I knew only too well because, in the past, many people had described me in the very same way.

Although I had never met Ted, and everything I knew about him was hearsay, I fell into the trap of making judgments about him. I believe that we sometimes see things in others that we don't like or can't accept in ourselves. And we end up disliking in others those same traits that we dislike in ourselves. I realized that I was doing this with Ted, that I was projecting on to him the things I did not like in myself.

At this point you may be wondering why I chose to write about someone for whom I initially had such mixed feelings. I picked Ted because in spite of the negative things I'd heard, he has demonstrated very powerfully how one person can make a difference in the world.

The many-windowed house of Ted's personality offers us numerous choices, and many possibilities to get sidetracked by any one of them. I learned many lessons from Ted, but perhaps one of the more important ones was not to be distracted by looking at only a single window at a time or at that window which has most recently been given the most attention. In this case, I have chosen to tell a little of his story by looking at Ted through the window of the heart.

Although I have not always believed this, today I believe that there is a light of love that shines in each of us. One way to rekindle our own light is to choose the window of love as we look upon others. If we do otherwise, and look at people through the windows of fear and judgment, our own love and creativity suffer.

Let me try to describe to you the particular window of Ted Turner that most powerfully attracted my attention. I met Ted at the Choices for the Future symposium in Aspen, Colorado, in 1987. This is an annual symposium sponsored by John Denver's Windstar organization. It attracts people from all over the world who are committed to improving our environment and making our world a more peaceful place in which to live.

When Ted addressed the symposium that day, he spoke from his heart, using no notes as he shared his complete and total commitment to bring peace to the world. There wasn't a hint of showmanship in his presentation, and his authenticity and integrity were very clear. I was so moved by his remarks, as was everyone there, that we gave him a standing ovation when he finished.

As I have gotten to know Ted better, I see him very differently than I once did, as I am viewing through a different window. What I see is a person who totally believes in himself and believes that nothing is impossible. He has demonstrated this even when he has been surrounded by people who believed the opposite was true and who perhaps even thought that his visions bordered on the insane.

I believe that his secret of success—whether in business, sailing, creating the Special Olympics games in the Soviet Union, in the tremendous support he has given the Cousteau project, or any one of his other projects—is his ability to commit every part of his being to his vision. He has learned to let go of the "doubting Thomas" that plagues so many of us. When I think about this, I realize that another reason why I chose Ted to be in this book is that he so beautifully demonstrates the wonderful capacities that can come alive within each of us when we don't allow any kind of negative feedback to deter us from our goals. Once Ted has the vision in his mind, he is able to keep that vision alive, focused like a laser beam, glowing with bright light. He seems able to refuse to let any darkness interfere with the clarity of the vision he has chosen.

Before going on to my interview with Ted, let me share with you just a few of his accomplishments. In 1970 he purchased Channel 17, an Atlanta independent UKHF television station. In December 1976, he originated the Super Station concept, transmitting the station's signal to cable systems nationwide via satellite.

In 1976, Ted purchased the Atlanta Braves baseball team, and in January 1977 he bought the Atlanta Hawks basketball team. On June 1, 1980, Ted inaugurated CNN, the world's first live, in-depth, round-the-clock all-news television network.

In March 1985, Ted and J.J. Ebaugh formed the Better World Society, a nonprofit organization dedicated to the production and international distribution of television programming on issues of critical importance. In 1986 he organized the Inaugural Good Will Olympic games in Moscow. He has received numerous awards for achievement as well as having won national and world sailing titles.

I invite you now to imagine that you are with us at Big Sur on March 12 1989, high on the rocky coastline overlooking the Pacific, where Ted, I, and our mutual friend J.J. Ebaugh have come to spend the day. It is a small home with a large living room that has huge windows looking out over one of the most spectacular views I have ever seen. What I liked best was the pathway that led to the top of a cliff where there was a bench looking out over the blue Pacific. It was a clear, warm day and being there felt like heaven to me. It was here that we were to do most of the interview.

We had started our day together at about 9:00 a.m., sharing breakfast, then later having lunch and dinner together. That day was an amazing experience for me, filled with many silences as we seemed to become at one with the majestic beauty all around us. I had seen Ted under many different circumstances, and he had stayed at my home in Tiburon, California, but I had never had the opportunity to share nature with him.

Throughout the time I spent with Ted, I caught myself thinking, several times, that perhaps the most important things we share in our communications are the silences, especially those moments when we are immersed in nature and feel the awe of its beauty and interconnectedness.

Before we had breakfast, Ted remembered that he had forgotten to get some groceries. As we drove down the hill in his Jeep, he suddenly put on the brakes, stopped, and jumped out. He picked up an empty beer can that someone had tossed out on the road, put it in a trash container in the back of his Jeep, then proceeded down to the small market where everyone knew Ted on a first name basis.

That single event told me more about Ted Turner than a thousand words could have done. It told me that here was a man who wasn't just talking about saving the environment; he was doing something about it, even in the simplest tasks, like picking up trash that others had left behind. In that single gesture, I recognized a consistency in what Ted Turner thought and what he did. I had tremendous respect for that.

After breakfast, on top of the cliff overlooking the ocean, I asked Ted, "Based on the experience of the struggles you have had in your life, what might you say to eighteen-year-olds who are about to go out into the world on their own? What can these young people learn from you about making a difference?"

Ted replied, "It's important to do good in order to make the world a little better, kinder, more thoughtful and caring place. There is a Helen Keller in just about every one of us. As far as my background is concerned, everything I saw, everything I read, and everything that happened to me influenced my life."

I asked Ted to tell me a little about his fantasies and daydreams as a child and something about those early years.

"I always loved the outdoors and I loved animals," Ted answered. "I would have been happy doing anything involved with wildlife and nature. I really liked that. As a young child I went to a very religious Presbyterian school where Evangelicals came in and preached to us about salvation and damnation. I was taken in by it.

"I was in military school from the time I was eleven until I was seventeen, when I began to wonder about religion. My sister got sick with lupus when I was fifteen, and I did a lot of praying to help her get well, but none of it did any good. Good Christians are not supposed to worry about not getting their prayers answered.

"You're not supposed to lose your faith when something awful happens to someone you love, but sometimes it does happen that way. My sister was three years younger than I. She was a real sweet little girl who became sick when she was twelve. She was ill for about five years before she passed away and the disease destroyed her mind and kept her from growing. She was just terribly sick all the time and was in tremendous pain.

"It was so heart-wrenching for us all that it just about destroyed my family. My parents eventually got divorced. My mother was running around trying to find miracle cures all over the world, but there were none. Even today, thirty years later, they still have no cure for lupus. All this really shook my religious faith."

I questioned Ted about his spiritual and religious beliefs and asked him if he had become an atheist after his sister's death.

"Well, I don't know if *atheist* is the right word. I have my own beliefs but I kind of like to keep them to myself. I don't ask people what their religious beliefs are. I don't like labels. I've got my beliefs, and they're private."

It was clear that Ted didn't wish to say more about this, so I changed the subject. "Who were the people who particularly influenced you in your early years?" I asked.

"My father probably had the greatest influence of any single person. He was basically really kind all the time, but he had his ideas about discipline, was a tough disciplinarian, and his ideas were very strong ones. He was from the old school. He believed most strongly about the things he believed in, and there was not much need to discuss those things. It was pretty hard to change his mind about anything."

I asked, "What do you think was the most important thing he taught you?"

"Several things come to mind. He taught me a very strong sense of honor. He was also very strong on good old-fashioned hard work. He believed that if a young person had it tough growing up, it would be easier on you when you got older. You would have learned how to handle adversity, hard work, independence, and so forth.

"That was one of the reasons he sent me to military school, so that I would learn to be strong and independent. You have to be strong and independent in the school where I went because you didn't have your parents to run to every time you had troubles. You have to work things out pretty much for yourself when you're at boarding school."

Although he had mentioned his parents' divorce, he hadn't gone into details, and I felt that it was really painful for him to talk about personal relationships. He seemed more willing to talk about his father's than his mother's influence on his life. The picture he described was that his mother was pretty much dominated by his father. Certainly we have all experienced traumas, fears, rejections, and disappointments in childhood. At this point in the interview I just didn't feel it was appropriate to press Ted about his early years. Although a lot of things seemed to be left unsaid, I did have the feeling that there was much potential for fear, bitterness, and lack of trust. His sister's death, a strict upbringing that did not have much expression of tenderness, and his being sent off to military school all contained the seeds for much grievance.

Although Ted could have allowed those bitter feelings to seep into every part of his life, he seemed satisfied to identify with what he saw as his father's most positive and important traits. Namely, he learned the discipline of believing in yourself one hundred percent, of believing that nothing is impossible, and not to let other people's beliefs deter you from your goal.

As I thought about Ted's relationship with his father, I was once again reminded that every experience we have in our lives, whether we first perceive it as good or bad, can be viewed as a positive lesson that the universe has given us. How liberating that realization has been in my life, to see that we really can choose, and that we do not have to look at the world through the prison window of our own bitterness over past grievances.

I asked Ted, "When you were in your twenties, what books particularly influenced you?"

Ted replied, "In those days I was interested in history and the classics. I wanted to be a success. I wanted to be rich and famous, and be a hero . . . that sort of thing. I wasn't thinking about what was best for the planet, yet. I was forty before I realized things were in such a mess."

Ted's words reminded me that it is never too late or too early to be awakened. Like Ted, in my youth I wasn't concerned with what was happening to the planet; my consciousness was focused only on what was happening to me. And yes, in those days, although I am not happy to admit it, I was the sort of person who did not give a second thought to throwing a little trash out my car window.

I mentioned to Ted that I had recently read a survey about today's college students that stated they are mostly interested in material things, how much money they can make, and how much power they can get. I asked him what his reflections were about that.

Ted responded quickly and spontaneously, "Making a good living and being financially successful is important everywhere. It is even important in the socialist countries. People want to provide for their families in a meaningful way. There are a lot of other things that are important, too, of course.

"During an average year," Ted went on, "I speak to probably ten or twelve colleges. I try to encourage young people to think about leading a life of service to mankind while being personally successful. The two don't have to conflict."

Ted Turner is one of the busiest people I know, but just as with so many busy, successful people I have been privileged to know, he has learned to prioritize his time. Making time to speak to young people is just one of his priorities. I have been present at a number of Ted's talks. Each time he speaks, he lights a fire in the hearts of everyone who hears him, inspiring them to care and do something to make a positive difference in our world.

Our conversation turned to the subject of making choices and decisions in our lives and of how important this is. Ted told me, "There is a saying, 'Be sure of your information, then go ahead.' My father was the first one who pointed this out to me, but it was not original with him. He taught me that when it is your life, you have got to make your own choices.

"If you have the confidence in yourself to make your own choices, you get all the information you can, along with the advice and counsel of people you think are wise. After you have done that, you have your own mind and you know the consequences. If it is your money and your business interests; you have to make the decisions. If they are wrong you will suffer for them; if they are right you will prosper."

I said, "In other words, you really have to believe in yourself one hundred percent. Get your facts and go for it and then not hang onto mistakes and wrong decisions."

"Right," Ted said. "I think that is a prerequisite for success in the long haul. Everyone who is doing anything at all will run into blind alleys and get off on a wrong track now and then. Everybody does. It is not possible to do otherwise; being able to bounce back from it is what makes a real champion.

"You should not make decisions until you have complete knowledge about things," he said. "But sometimes you have to form opinions without as much information as you should have, or without firsthand knowledge. When that's the case, you should not have hard and fast opinions. Then, when new information becomes available, you should be able to change your mind. That has been very valuable for me. I have been able to change my mind, and I think all of us who are trying to reach understanding and true wisdom have got to have open, flexible minds. We are learning things so quickly these days. If you have set opinions about things, you cannot progress."

Ted seemed to become more and more thoughtful as he spoke, looking out over the ocean as though it was the source of his inspiration. "The thing that really helped me a lot about making decisions was sailing," he said. "When you're sailing a boat in competition, you can go either to the left or to the right. But you just have to make decisions, one way or the other, the whole time you are in the race. You have to make split-second decisions about whether to pull sail or let it out. These are mental decisions, as opposed to physical decisions, like in playing tennis, that you make so quickly. My mind is not quick enough to make that many physical decisions, but sailing is really a very cerebral sport and I started doing it when I was ten years old.

"Other things that helped me learn how to make decisions were chess, which I played a lot, and Monopoly, bridge, and other card games. You have to make a lot of decisions when you play bridge and poker. The new electronic games don't require decision-making ability. They require physical dexterity more than mental quickness. You have to be quick but you don't have to be analytical."

Some time passed as we sat back and enjoyed the ocean view. I remembered a story I'd heard about Ted firing someone who he learned had been disloyal to him. I began to wonder how Ted let go of old grievances with people who had wronged him in business or elsewhere. "How do you deal with that?" I asked.

"It's hard to forgive when someone you trust stabs you in the back or embezzles funds, or something like that. The legal phrase for it is 'larceny after trust.' On the other hand, you expect your competitors to try to best you any way they can. But when someone who is supposed to be on the same team as you betrays you, that is the hardest thing I find to forgive."

Ted reminded me that to have inner peace we need to learn to see the value of forgiveness. He also talked about what our egos want us to believe—that it is not always easy to forgive those who we feel have hurt us or did not honor the trust we placed in them.

In my own struggles with the forgiveness process, I could sympathize with Ted's struggles to let go of grievances, and I think this is a lifelong process for all of us. I believe that many of us, like Ted, feel the value of forgiving and we know that unforgiving thoughts do not really bring us the peace of mind that we inwardly seek.

I asked Ted what famous people had influenced him. He responded: "I would say that of the people I never met, Gandhi and Martin Luther King were most important. They were tremendous heroes of mine in the battle for peace. But there are many others: Captain Cousteau and his son John Michael; Russel Peterson, who is the head of the Audubon Society; Lester Brown, the head of Worldwide Institute.

"All these people have had a lot to do with my becoming an active participant in the battles for peace, for a clean environment, for population control, and for stopping the arms race."

I believe that if we wish to break the barriers of our self-imposed limitations, it can be very helpful to have models like Ted who themselves have broken them. I believe that in a psychological and spiritual sense, every person who has broken barriers is an ordinary person who has done extraordinary things. They have put on wings, and with the wind of love under them have soared high to show us a new way. They teach us that we can do the same.

I told Ted, "I heard you speak at Choices for the Future a couple years ago. And I heard you speak in Washington, D.C., at the Soviet-American summit meeting. What comes through loud and clear is your compassion and your love for this planet and all that is living on it. What comes through like a bolt of lightning is your total commitment to these causes. There are many people who are interested in the environment but not that interested. What can a person do to help light that kind of fire and passion you have?"

Ted then became very animated, talking with tremendous zeal. "This planet is my home! It is our home. People don't think about it that way. People think of their little house and little yard and their little town as their home. That was fine two hundred years ago! But the world has shrunk and shrunk and shrunk. One of the things that changed our thinking was the first photographs that came back from outer space. We saw that the world was truly round and very, very small. Each individual person is tiny. We saw that this is a small and frail place. It is like a person's flower garden.

"All it takes is a poison spray and you can kill your whole garden in ten minutes. Basically, that is what we are doing with the earth. We are spraying chemicals all over it to increase food production, for example.

"We are wrecking our home, that's all. There are a great many people worried about these things, and I am one of them. We have got to change. Nobody wants to spread poison in their yard. Nobody wants to feed poisoned food to their children or give their families water that isn't fit to drink.

"Everybody wants clean water, and clean air. Everybody wants a yard free of garbage. But they don't worry about the garbage being in someone else's yard, or someone else's water or air being poisoned. Well, that's got to change. We have to develop a global ethic, not just a personal ethic."

Just at this moment we both became tremendously excited as we spotted a huge whale rising to the surface of the ocean and blowing a towering geyser of water from its spout. We then saw another whale, and still another.

It was such a beautiful sight I almost couldn't believe that I could be so fortunate. Both Ted and I marveled at this spectacular picture of nature that it was our gift to witness. Without saying it, I sensed that we both felt our words were mundane at this precious moment, and we both instantly stopped the interview and dropped into a meditative silence of awe and appreciation.

After several moments Ted turned to me and asked to continue, and I responded by asking him, "When did you first start developing your global perspective?"

"It was a gradual process. I always loved the natural world. I have always been amazed by it. I used to watch the Cousteau programs and the National Geographic specials. Cousteau started saying these things years ago. I also read Rachel Carson's books. In my mind these two people are the mother and father of modern conservation. I read *The Club of Rome* and *The Limits of Growth*, and when Carter was president I read *The Global Two Thousand Report*. From then on I listened to a lot of different people and different programs and read a lot of books and articles.

"Every year the World Watch Institute publishes a book on the health of the planet, about air pollution, acid rain, soil erosion, armaments, health care and education. It is called *The State of the World*, and I read it every year. I recommend it strongly to everyone. Also, there is a book which was published last year called *Our Common Future*. It reports on a commission, underwritten by the United Nations, to take a look at global problems and what can be done about them."

Here, once again, Ted became a teacher for me. If a busy person like Ted can make it a point to keep himself informed, then, I thought, maybe I'd better stop making excuses and rationalizing that in my life I just don't have time to keep up with these things.

Because of Ted, I read *Our Common Future*, by the prime minister of Norway, Gro Harlem Brundtland. It would be difficult to read that book and not want to become a global citizen. Yet, I do not think I am alone in the apathy I once had toward the problems of the environment. So much of the time, it seems that we are too busy to take time to discuss problems such as acid rains or the destruction of the rain forests. Perhaps we can all look to Ted as a teacher, listening to our hearts and making it a top priority to keep better informed on the environmental issues that face us. Then we can start to do something about it ourselves, rather than ignoring it or waiting for others to act.

I asked Ted, "What is your vision for the future? What things would you like to see accomplished during your lifetime?"

"I'd like to see us turn it around. The planet is like a big sports franchise that is having trouble. It needs a change of management. I think that the leadership in the Soviet Union is more progressive than any they have had since the Revolution. But it is a leadership focused mainly on the here and now, rather than on global and long-term problems.

"We have nearly two hundred different countries on this planet and each one has different problems. The three greatest problems that we all face are the arms race, increasing population, particularly in the Third World countries, and the degradation of the environment. These are extraordinarily complex problems, requiring total involvement from every country.

"In my opinion, it is going to require tremendous strengthening of the United Nations. We have to start dealing with these problems on a global basis. It's going to require a change in the way we think and do things. In the past, we felt that only the success of the United States was important, and somehow we were competing with the entire world.

"To some extent we are competing with the rest of the world but I feel that we have had a superiority complex, thinking that we are better than other people and are entitled to live better. We are a rich country but that kind of thinking isn't going to fly anymore. One of the things that Captain Cousteau said that really touched me was that when there are poor people in other parts of the world living in abject poverty, it is impossible to fully enjoy your own life, knowing that so many people have nothing.

"So, we have to work to make things better for everyone. That doesn't necessarily mean that we have to give up things so that others can have more. It can be done partially through technology, but it must be with the proper use of technology. Too much of the world's financial resources and brain power are going into the creation and maintenance of armaments. The world military budget is now a trillion dollars per year."

I said, "The world sees you as a guy who is very powerful and who can be pretty rough at times. Yet you spend as much time as anyone I know helping to improve our relationship with the Soviet Union. What are some of the ways we can break the barriers to improve friendship and cooperation and a sense of global citizenry?"

Without a moment's hesitation Ted replied, "First you must start thinking like a global citizen. Do a little studying and reach your own conclusions. There are no bad people on this planet. The only things that are bad are bad environments and bad teaching.

"A perfect example of this was how they treated little children in Germany and Japan prior to World War II. They taught them militarism from the time they were born. They taught them to swear loyalty to the Fuhrer and to die for the Emperor. Think of it this way: the same children could have been taught to be either Eagle Scouts or Hitler Youth. It was just a question of what you taught them."

As we were looking out over the ocean we saw another group of whales go by. As we had done before, we stopped the interview and enjoyed another long interval of silence as they passed by.

I then asked Ted, "What about responsibility in our

personal rela:ionships? Do you have any thoughts about the importance of taking responsibility for healing relationships in our own lives?"

I wasn't prepared for Ted to quote the Bible, but this is exactly what he did. "It says in the Bible that you should forgive your enemies. That is one of the things you have got to do. You have to learn how not to harbor a grudge, how to forgive.

"We [our country] did that. We forgave the Germans and Japanese after World War II, and I think it is one of the reasons we haven't had another war with them. We gave them a hand and helped them up from defeat. We didn't grind them into the ground the way the Allies did with Germany after World War I. They had to pay tremendous reparation and they were humiliated. There was a lot of hatred and resentment on the part of the German people for the way they were treated after their defeat.

"Hitler grew up in an atmosphere where there was a lot of hatred, and he became the leader of their country. As long as there are people like that, I guess we will need police forces. Maybe we will someday have a system around the world where leaders are picked who are qualified and kind and wise. I think it is really important to do this. Humanity must pick leaders who can set new courses of action for us, toward a sustainable society."

I asked, "What are your thoughts about women in leadership roles?"

Ted replied, "Women have not been offered the opportunities that men have had. As we become a more cerebral society, women are being offered greater opportunities. It is still not easy for women, particularly if they choose to have children. More and more women are moving into leadership roles, and I think that is good."

Now I wanted to ask Ted a very different kind of question. I told him that I felt that one of our greatest fears is our fear of death. I asked, "Do you feel death is a reality or a kind of transition to another kind of existence? What are your thoughts about this?"

"I would agree that most people fear death. I don't want to die, but I am aware that we all must die. I don't know what's going to happen after I am gone. I would love to think that there is a beautiful heaven up in the clouds, where we all would be par golfers, and those who like to fish, as I do, would catch big fat trout on every cast.

"But that would be dull, wouldn't it? My personal wish would be for an afterlife like the one the Indians believed in, that there is a happy hunting ground. Maybe there is such a place. Otherwise, there is a lot of energy in each one of us and at the very least our bodies get recycled back into the environment."

After a prolonged silence, he continued, "Maybe it just returns to wherever it came from. What's so bad about that?"

"After you have left your body and are no longer on the planet in a physical form," I asked, "what would you like people to say about you and the contribution you have made?"

It was as if Ted's response was on his lips even before I had finished the question. "I try to look at things from a galactic standpoint, seeing that we are just tiny people in a little planet off in the corner of the universe. That is not to belittle what we are trying to do, but against the backdrop of cosmic time, what we really do does not make a whole lot of difference.

"But that doesn't mean that we don't work hard to try and make this a better place. Those who are helping others and are concerned about the larger issues seem happier, more content than those who are just seeking their own selfish pleasures."

Since I was struggling to find more balance in my own life, and trying not to put so many things on my platter at the same time, I asked Ted, "How do you get balance in your life? Here we are, at this moment, enjoying one of the most beautiful views in the world, looking out over the Pacific Ocean. We have seen seals and sea otters playing, and have been sustained by the beauty of nature this day. But how do you handle the struggles on a day-to-day basis, and how do you bring balance into your life? Does prayer or meditation play a part in your life?"

Ted answered, "No, I don't meditate. I do some thinking. I work like the devil during the week and I commune with nature on the weekends. I get my kicks looking at things on this planet—the animals, birds, insects, fish, flowers and the trees. I like to see people, too. I think people are really neat, but I think the other things are neat too."

I then asked one of my favorite questions: "Of all the many things you are doing right now, what excites you the most?"

"I am very excited about every project I'm working on," Ted replied. "Of the television projects, the one I think has the most potential, and I am happiest about the way it is developing, is *The World Report*, which we run on Sundays, where we get the news from all over the world.

"I think we have some ninety countries participating in that. We hope to have all the countries on Earth participating before too much longer."

Because of my lifelong work with children, I felt a need to ask, "How do we teach children to see themselves as global citizens rather than as citizens of one country or another? Can this be done through the schools?"

Ted told me, "We are running a series of programs we call *Ports of the Soviet Union*. It is a seven-hour look at the Soviet Union. Televison can be a great influence on children. So we try to get videotapes from these programs into the schools so that more of these issues are in the curriculum."

I mentioned that we had not talked very much about A Better World Society, which Ted helped to develop and get off the ground. "Would you share with us what that organization is about and what you would like to accomplish with it?"

Ted replied eagerly, "I was despairing over the fact that we were doing some hard-hitting documentaries but could not get advertisers to underwrite them. Advertisers were not interested in hard-hitting documentaries on birth control, nuclear weapons, or the environment. Then J.J. and I were talking about it and she suggested that we start an organization that would get funding from other philanthropic groups and from individuals who were interested in helping to fund these programs. That was the idea that got the Better World Society started."

What Ted did not say that day, but which I knew as a fact, was that he had contributed the original seed money for this organization to get off the ground.

Ted, J.J. and I had been together on several different occasions before, in both formal and informal settings. It became clear to me that the friendship they shared was a powerful and important one for both of them. J.J. Ebaugh is a most extraordinary, gentle person who is awakened to the knowledge that she is on a spiritual pathway and has a very close relationship to God. She is as intelligent, energetic and effervescent as she is beautiful, a most amazing person with a great variety of accomplishments, talents and abilities, not the least of which are being an excellent commercial airplane pilot, a competitive sailer and a race car driver. Like Ted, J.J. is determined to make a difference in the world, and so it is not surprising to me that they have worked together to form the Better World Society.

I thought it would be interesting to explore Ted's relationship with his children, and when I thought about them it occurred to me that their dad could be an awfully hard act to follow. I imagined that as a father Ted could be demanding. I mentioned to him that we hadn't talked about his relationships with his children and his hopes for them.

In a very gentle and soothing tone, speaking quite slowly, which was quite different from his usual machine-gun quickness of speech, he said, "The most important thing that ever happened to me was becoming a parent. I love my children very much and I am very proud of them.

"I have three boys and two girls. They are all young adults now, the oldest twenty-six and the youngest eighteen. One of the things that I most regret is that we don't spend as much time together as I'd like. Two are in college, two are out of college, and one is graduating from high school this year. Only one of them is married. I see them whenever I can, and we are close."

Perhaps that was a fitting note to wrap up the interview, speaking of the love for one's children and our belief in them and the future. Ted and I spent the rest of the day relaxing, and as the sun began to set we enjoyed a quiet dinner together.

I had a very special experience as the evening came to an end. I was thinking of what a writer's paradise this home of Ted's would be when, as if he had read my mind he said, "Jerry, if you ever want to use this place to write, just give us a jingle on the phone.

Unfortunately, we don't get here too often." Well, that put a smile on my face and in my heart.

Afterword

I almost have to laugh at myself as I remember my first feelings about Ted, which were ambivalent, to say the least. I had heard stories that he was so rough and tough that he ate nails for breakfast. Although I knew this had to be an exaggeration, there was a part of me that was fearful and thought maybe he would chew me up and spit me out. It is amazing how our fears can limit us when we succumb to other people's perceptions.

I know that there are many other stories that might be told about Ted Turner, but I am glad that I chose the window I did for this interview. By choosing the window of love, I was able to let go and transform some of the negative pictures I had of Ted.

It continues to fascinate me how, when we choose to see people in the present and not allow their pasts to cast shadows of judgment over our perceptions, we discover the essence of love and caring that always abides in the present.

As I reflect on the feelings I had when I began this interview, I have to be honest, it was more than ambivalence that I had toward Ted. The truth is, I really didn't like him, in spite of all the wonderful things I knew he had done. As I look back at it now, I see that my mind was being led by my ego, and I was more concerned with the things Ted had done in the past that were not so admirable.

What a wonderful sense of freedom it is to know that we do not have to be stuck in the past, and to know that love is our only reality. It is the only reality we have because only it is eternal.

It is very rare that Ted grants interviews. It is not something he likes to do. So, as it turns out, we both had some negative feelings going into the interview. I know that I had a personal transformation that day. It was a magical day for me and I hope there was a little magic in it for Ted.

And now I can tell you, with absolute sincerity and honesty, that I not only like this guy Ted Turner I feel great love for him, glad that we are sharing this planet.

7

DR. GEORGE
WOOD

Love is the way I walk in gratitude.

Dr. Wood taught me that you don't have to make a big splash to make a difference in this world. I became acquainted with this man after reading a heartwarming story in the newspaper about a very special birthday party that was being given in his honor. The party was to be held in the small community of St. Helena, California, where Dr. Wood had practiced medicine since 1925. The occasion being celebrated was the doctor's ninety-first birthday, but it was to be much more than that. It would turn out to be a party to top all parties.

But before telling you about the party, I would like to tell you a little bit about Dr. Wood himself. You see, he had served the people of St. Helena as a general practitioner for sixty-one years, and in that time he had delivered over two thousand babies. It was these babies who were giving him his ninety-first birthday party, and that is what made it so very special.

What really touched my heart was that many of these babies, now adults, came from all over the country to pay tribute to this special man. I loved the fact that Dr. Wood's "babies" lined up at the party to be reintroduced. There were prizes for the oldest mother present, for the most generations delivered by Dr. Wood, for the oldest twins, for the first born and the last born, and for the person who had traveled the greatest distance to honor Dr. Wood this day.

There was a most wonderful parade as all the babies Dr. Wood had delivered marched in formation, divided up according to the decade in which they were born. The master of ceremonies asked the audience of more than a thousand people how many of them had been delivered by Dr. Wood. More than two hundred hands went up.

The local newspaper, *The St. Helena Star*, stated that "premium wine put St. Helena on the map, but Dr. George Wood put it on the front page—and on network television and the radio."

When it came time to blow out the candles on his cake, Dr. Wood presented a short speech, stating simply, "With all the changes in the valley and the world, with all the stress and conflict, it is friends that really make the difference." He went on to speak of his commitment to the education of young people and of the importance of helping others.

As a medical doctor, Dr. Wood had often provided family medical care free of charge to those who could not afford to pay for his services. In 1984, he received recognition for his generosity when he was given the Frederick Plessner Memorial Award for outstanding service as a country doctor.

Many years before Dr. Wood retired, he and his wife set up a scholarship fund and gave away thousands of dollars to students in need of financial help for college. They had given this money anonymously so that no one who received it would feel any obligation. I learned, in reading about Dr. Wood, that he had also given many thousands of dollars to the St. Helena Public Library building fund, making it a community resource that people of all ages could enjoy.

When I first heard the story of Dr. Wood's life, there

was something in the very center of my soul that knew I just had to meet this man. For me he represented a rare jewel, a person who was living his life with total commitment, authenticity, integrity, dependability, and trust. Here was a person who really loved and cared about people. I wanted to meet him because it was my wish that some of the essence of this gentle man would rub off on me.

On my first meeting with Dr. Wood, I thought that whoever had made up the word *gentleman* must have somehow had this man in mind. What struck me immediately was what might have seemed a contradiction but was not. Although he was shy, at the same time he was a real "live wire," filled with zest, curiosity, and wonderment. He gave me the impression that all his senses were wide open to receive new experiences. He was so totally alive and full of energy that I kept forgetting his age.

As I learned about his life, and then spoke with him, I realized that the ideals by which he lived were the ones I so much wanted to live by in my own life, yet for me each day seemed filled with temptations and challenges that acted like magnets, tugging me away from my intended course. Here was a man who had established a steady course for his life and had managed to maintain it. Additionally, he seemed ageless, as if he had learned of a way to escape the usual hazards of aging.

Here was a person whom I felt privileged to interview, and I hoped I would find out what made him tick. It occurred to me that there were so many things in his character that could be models for others, including me.

He did not give the appearance of a man in his nineties, and it was clear that his heart was still centered with the youth and enthusiasm of a child. He was a very short man, yet when he stood up he seemed seven feet tall. For me, and I think for many others close to him, Dr. Wood had heroic stature. If John Wayne had walked into the room, I swear the doctor would have seemed to tower over him. For me, he was living proof that contributing something positive in life and really making a difference in this world does not depend on the size of your body, how big your muscles are, or how much noise you make. I was so impressed that Dr. Wood had not been limited by the belief systems of so many others around him and that he had found his own definitions of what it took to have both inner and outer success in life.

One of the subjects we talked about was physical size and how it had affected his life. Dr. Wood confided that all through his ninety-one years he had received many lessons because of his size. When he was a boy and a young adult, he had been self-conscious about being small, and he had suffered many painful emotional wounds and low self-esteem before he came to terms with this fact of his life.

"As a small kid, life wasn't easy," he said. "Let's face it, if you weighed enough to play football, if your legs were long enough to run fast at track, a young man could do something that others his age felt was worthwhile. I guess it seemed there wasn't much I could do. I didn't quite learn how to take care of my feelings about it [his size] until I was in the Navy, in World War I.

"At the time I didn't appreciate it, but there was one of the members of the Navy Flying Corps, a man about six foot, who weighed about a hundred ninety pounds. He called me a 'little shrimp,' and it hurt. I never thought much about it, but this fellow taught me a lesson."

Dr. Wood explained that this was certainly not the

first time that he had been called a "little shrimp," but this time it had been especially painful. He became very angry at the person who had called him this, yet he did not stay attached to either his anger or his pain. He told me that he suddenly came to realize that he couldn't change his physical body. But he also knew that he was much more than his physical body and there were things he could do to live a life that he felt was worthwhile.

Dr. Wood told me, "I never *consciously* thought a lot about all this, but I recognize that the experience remained in my guts and in my heart. I learned that it was not the size of your body that counts in this world, but what mattered was how much caring and love you contributed. It made me think more seriously about life and what I could contribute."

As I saw how this mild-mannered man had enriched the community in which he lived, I was reminded of my own childhood and young adulthood. In those days I, and many others, thought you had to be big and muscular, strong, outspoken, and make a big splash in order to get things done and really affect the world.

Like Dr. Wood, I had been painfully aware that the world I lived in valued men according to how competitive, how large they were. Being the youngest in my family, my parents had always called me "the baby." I didn't like that, and I remember wanting to be as tall as or taller than my two brothers.

In those days there weren't any Rambos, but in many popular magazines there were pictures of a man by the name of Charles Atlas. His body bulged with muscles. Magazine ads promised the readers that we could be like Charles Atlas if we just followed his exercise program.

The big carrot motivating adolescent boys to send away for this program was the promise of having every girl on the beach after them. The ad had a cartoon of a skinny, unhappy little guy all alone on the beach while another man, with bulging muscles, was surrounded by beautiful young women.

I remember falling for this ad. I sent away for it and for a while I did the exercises it showed. But my muscles never looked like Charles Atlas's, and I continued to be that lonely, skinny little guy with no girl friends, trying to find his own barely visible biceps. Unlike Dr. Wood, for a long time I felt that the size of my body very much limited what I could contribute to the world.

It quickly became clear that one of the many lessons Dr. Wood taught was that it was not the size of your muscles that counted so much as the size of your heart and how much love you gave to others.

Dr. Wood told me, "I went into medicine even though there were no doctors in my family. I went into it with the idea that I could do something with it. I wanted to really do something in this world that was worthwhile, and I was not going to be limited by any other person's evaluation of me."

As I thought about these words, I realized that I still need teachers like Dr. Wood in my life, because too often I succumb to the belief that who I am is dependent on what others think of me. It is often difficult for me to allow my self-esteem to be determined only by my own evaluation of who I am.

Too often I have felt that my self-worth depends on how many professional papers I have published or my status on a hospital staff, or whether I had the title of "instructor" or "professor." That day, Dr. Wood reminded me that who we are does not depend on what others think, but on the values and thoughts we have about ourselves. He also reminded me that we gain humility when we know who we are inside and no longer require recognition and assurance from others.

In the world today, I do not think it is possible to learn too much about humility. Dr. Wood's humility reminded me of a time when my son Lee and I were in India and were invited by Mother Teresa to travel with her as she gave several lectures. At that time Lee was just finishing up his doctorate in psychology and had a most relevant question to ask Mother Teresa. "What do you think are the most important traits for a person to have in the healing professions?" he asked.

Mother Teresa's reply was both quick and simple: "Humility and meekness." This answer stirred me to my very toes. I immediately thought about both Lee's education and my own. These two traits that Mother Teresa put at the top of her list were rarely taught in the schools that trained people in the healing professions.

As Dr. Wood and I sat talking in his home that day, I could not help but notice how warm and neat it was. Everything seemed very old, indeed. What was most important for me to experience, however, was the quiet expansiveness of love that seemed to fill the house. There was no question that I was in a home where love had been experienced at its fullest, and I could almost hear its song of love in every room I entered.

It was my impression that Dr. Wood's inner fulfillment and satisfaction had not come from the accolades of other people, or from being famous, or from being the author of many books. Rather, his had been a life of expanding his heart by giving to others while seeking nothing in return. I could not help but look at my own life and at the lives of so many of my colleagues. I recognized how often so many of us are driven by the desire to perform and how we hand over to others the power to decide whether we are worthwhile individuals. Even when giving to others, we seem to get caught up in "giving in order to get," where there is the goal or expectation that we are somehow going to be rewarded.

When I asked Dr. Wood about the scholarships he and his wife had given anonymously, he told me, "I gave it with the idea that many youngsters needed financial help to get through school, and I felt that they shouldn't feel any obligations with it, that they would just get it and use it for their educations." He went on to say that perhaps the experience of receiving help might, at a later time in their lives, give the recipients of these scholarships the motivation to experience the joy of helping someone else.

In attempting to discover more about Dr. Wood's inner world and his motivations for giving money to the local library, I asked, "Why did you choose to give money for building a library?"

He thought about his answer for quite some time, then answered very simply, "People enjoy it. I was at the bank today and a lady who works there told me, 'You know, we were talking about the town and the things for kids to do. My boy, after he finishes school, thinks it's wonderful to go over to the library, and I pick him up when I finish work and we go home together. My brother-in-law, who had polio when he was a child, has to use a wheelchair, and he can wheel himself in and so forth.' So the library, I think, has done a good deal for the people of the community."

Later, when I asked him how many babies he estimated he had delivered in all the years of his practice, he answered, "I tried to count it up and I thought I probably delivered about two thousand babies. I was delivering pretty close to a hundred a year there for about ten years, and I delivered as many as four babies in twenty-four hours."

Despite having delivered that many babies, spread over a sixty-year period, it was rumored that he could

146

look at a person's picture and say, "Oh, I know that person's name!" and then could tell you something about the person's life. It seemed as if he continued to feel joined with the lives of all the people he'd ever touched in his long life as a doctor in the community.

I told him about this rumor and I asked him if there was any truth in it. Was he really able to look at a photograph of a person and tell you that person's name, even when the photograph was taken many years after he had last treated that person?

"I think it is exaggerating a bit," he said. "But really, I can tell many of them."

We then began talking about the big birthday party they'd had for him. With a look of delight on his face that seemed to radiate a wonderful light through the whole room where we were sitting, he told me, "People came from Oregon, Washington, Colorado, Arizona, from the East, the South, and just about all over the United States."

"It must have warmed your heart to know that so many people love you," I said, thinking of how far many of these people had traveled, leaving their jobs and their families, just to give of themselves and to be present at what they must have felt was an important commemoration.

"Yes, it does," he replied. "You can't get away from it. The people would come just to give me a good celebration. It was the nicest thing you could possibly have happen to you."

I wondered if there could be anything more important and more joyous than having an opportunity to say thank you to a man whose life has been dedicated, with so much love, to the service of his community!

I paused for a moment and thought that every one of us must have had people in our lives who loved and helped us along our life paths. I also thought how wonderful it would be if every now and then we called or wrote a note of love and thanks and acknowledgment to these people, letting them know how they had made a difference in our lives. No matter how troubled we might feel, it would surely bring a smile to our own faces and to the faces of the people we thanked.

I asked Dr. Wood to tell me a little more about his life. I wondered about his early years and how they had affected him. I wanted to know what influences had gone into creating in this man such an open and giving outlook on life.

"For my first twelve years," he said, "I lived on a ranch in North Dakota. It didn't offer very much. We went to town once or twice a year, rarely more than that. We went to a country school and I guess I had five or six years of grammar school there. My mother taught me before that.

"We came to California in 1908. I had two years of grammar school there, before going on to high school. We had a grain ranch and a fair herd of sheep. You would classify my first years as a ranch life, but very primitive ranch life."

As he spoke, he gave me the impression that his mother had been very important in encouraging him in pursuing the kinds of interests he would have in his adult years. I asked him if he could tell me a little bit about her and about the influence that both his parents had had on him.

"She had a good education," Dr. Wood said, "much more than my dad did. She did most of the teaching. But my dad read very extensively and he could tell you every character in every book he read . . . Shakespeare and some of the books he knew . . . so he really took advantage of his reading, too."

Since Dr. Wood had grown up in a rather isolated farming area many miles from the nearest town, he had no formal religious training, yet he had lived a life of caring and giving to others, which suggested that there was a very spiritual side to this man. I asked him about this.

At first he became thoughtful and a little shy, saying, "I have different views than others, and I don't think . . ." He paused. It seemed that he was searching for something to say that would be of benefit to other people who might read about him. Finally he said, "I think prayer is one of the most important things there is, but I think it's what it does for the individual. It makes you think of things and go over them. Prayer gives you better insight."

"Can you explain that a little more? You see, most of my life I was an atheist," I confessed. "It's been only since 1975 that I've turned to God, so I'm very interested in hearing what you might have to say."

Dr. Wood replied, "I can't go along with the preacher's hell and damnation and all this and that and the other thing. My philosophy is . . . I have my little contribution to make—and maybe it will help make this world a better place to live in. My point is, if I can do something that will make this a better place, that is the answer. I think you have to practice, not just preach."

And right there I found myself thinking that Dr. Wood had said, in a nutshell, what others have taken volumes to tell. Dr. Wood confirmed some of my own beliefs, that there is a difference between professing religious principles and theology and demonstrating and living those principles in our everyday lives. To me he is a most wonderful example of a man whose actions in the world speak louder than his words. He did not have a lot of words to say, but he had done much to make this a better world in his lifetime.

Dr. Wood had never been the kind of person who

tries to change the world by forcing others to fit into his mold. He was not the kind who was out there attacking others for what he might have believed was "wrong thinking." I saw in him a man who knew that the best teachers are always students, learning something new from everyone they meet.

What touched me very deeply was that throughout his life he had always done his best, in his small yet most significant way, to make a difference by living a life of love, caring, and nonjudgment. Through the example of his own joy, tranquility, and zest for life he demonstrated most dramatically what living a simple, dedicated life is all about. As we spoke that day, he described what perhaps is the cornerstone of his belief system: he begins each day by quieting his mind in prayer and communicating with God.

"A lot of people go into medicine wanting to help people," I said. "At the same time, making a lot of money also becomes very important to them. But money seemed less important to you than loving and caring for your patients. It seems that your whole life was one of loving and caring for your patients, as if they were your very own family rather than only your patients."

"I do love and care for them," he replied. "I think my personal touch mattered. It wasn't that I was so brilliant, because I wasn't. But I studied and worked as hard as any doctor I know. My practice was a very personal one."

As he spoke, I couldn't help but think about the many, many doctors I knew who had specialized in one area of medicine or another, men and women who were outstanding scientists and famous in their fields of expertise. But I had known so few who were able to give the caring and the love that were so important in the contribution that Dr. Wood had made.

It seemed to me that Dr. Wood was a specialist in his own right—in the area of personal communications. He was a specialist in love and caring, where the patient and physician spoke to each other on a heart-to-heart basis. I was certain no one felt like an object or a case number in Dr. Wood's practice, but rather they felt like a friend or family member. Dr. Wood may not have become an outstanding scientist, but he did become a specialist extraordinaire in caring for others and giving his love. Sometimes when we are trying to help another person we forget that love is the most powerful healing force in the world.

I asked Dr. Wood, "What allowed your heart to be so open, so that you were able to touch so many people? What did you learn in life to get that feeling of touching other people's hearts?"

"I think the one answer I have is that everybody you see should be important to you. Just what makes you feel that way, I can't answer. But to me this is important, there's no question about it. There are friends and people here, who are now in their sixties and seventies, who I saw when they were teenagers. No argument, they still mean a lot to me and I think I mean something to them."

Dr. Wood recalled a Founder's Day banquet at the University of California Medical School in San Francisco, where he was presented with an award for his life's work. In receiving the award, he gave a short thank-you speech to the people who honored him that day. He told me about what he had said in that speech, that we need to teach the children to make it a better world. We need to teach truth, honesty, kindness, tolerance, humility, and the Golden Rule, "Do unto others as you would have them do unto you."

In just those few seconds, Dr. Wood had spelled out a prescription for life that was practical, simple, and easily within everyone's grasp. He not only spelled it out but he lives the way of life he describes. The big question, of course, is that if those principles are so simple and practical, then why is it so often difficult for me—and so many others—to put these principles into practice?

I believe that the answer, in part, is that our egos like our minds to be confused and in a state of chaos. Too often we seem to convince ourselves that if something is simple, it just won't work.

I spoke with Dr. Wood about many different subjects. What deeply impressed me about him was that here was a man who was ninety-one years of age, who continued to have a great deal of caring and love for people. Although he no longer practiced medicine full-time, he still kept up to date on the diseases, treatments, and social issues that affect everyone in our world today.

Because of my own interest in AIDS, I asked Dr. Wood about this terrible disease that has touched the lives of so many thousands of people in our society.

He stated that he has great respect and concern for both the health and the rights of individuals. He was concerned about the disease and demonstrated in his conversation that he was well informed about it. One of the things that worried him was the issue of forced testing for AIDS in the workplace and the general community. He was very much against forced testing, saying that it was a violation of a person's individual rights. As we spoke, I was very impressed with how he had kept up with the complicated medical issues affecting us all today.

Our conversation turned to politics. It was an election year and Dr. Wood had many things to say about the presidential candidates and how their policies might affect our country and the rights of every individual living here. We talked about the welfare system, the defense budget, and how we might do away with nuclear weapons. I noticed that every opinion he gave reflected his love and concern for the individual and his belief that every one of us can contribute something to make this a better world in which to live.

At one point I asked him, "If there was a gathering of children right here in your living room, what advice or what wisdom would you like to share with them?"

He paused for only a moment. "I think I would probably say, love your fellow man. Do unto others as you would have them do unto you. Again, see if you can't make this a better world to live in. I would encourage them to live a natural life. Enjoy your work. Enjoy your play. Enjoy health by taking care of it on the sunny side of life."

Here Dr. Wood brought in a very important concept that could benefit so many of us. There are still many people, myself included, who became workaholics and forgot to enjoy playing. We became too engrossed in the dark side rather than the light side of life. We took life much too seriously and forgot that being playful, joyful, and laughing at ourselves, even daring to be silly, can be a most important part of life.

Dr. Wood spoke of how important it was to choose to look at the sunny side of life, to be an optimist rather than a pessimist, to think positively, not negatively, in spite of what might happen.

In commenting on the last point, I asked Dr. Wood, "How do you look at the sunny side of life when you see all around you a world filled with so much tragedy and sadness?"

"I think you have to look at this, analyze it, and say, if you get depressed, what good does it do? First, you feel down and poor. Second, everybody you see begins to feel the same way. So what do you accomplish, and do you ever get over it that way? I think you have to do the things you can in life, so that you can see there are pleasant things out there."

Being in the presence of this man, who had given so much to his many, many patients and friends over the years, it was difficult to think of him as ever having any enemies. I asked, "Do you still hold on to any grievances against anybody in your life?"

His answer was immediate and firm: "I don't hold any grievances against anyone."

"In your life," I said, "you have spent a lot of time loving people, animals, plants, and nature, and all of the things that are God's gifts to humanity. It is clear that it has been very important for you to demonstrate our oneness with life. Has religion in any way played a role in shaping your beliefs?"

"I would say that it definitely played a role. Yes, it makes a certain difference in my attitude toward individuals and my outlook on life."

Next I asked him if he had any particular advice to parents.

"Well," he said, "I think you have to be firm, but I think making those kids feel that they are an important part of the family, to listen to them and to see if they wish to share some of the problems they have—probably this is the best answer I know."

He paused for a moment, then added, "The other answer is to be an example for them."

I mentioned to him that many physicians put their practices before their families, and this often becomes a problem. Dr. Wood very quickly told me that his practice always came first and his wife never objected to this. Whenever the telephone rang and it was one of his patients, his wife supported him in his mission to serve them.

He described a relationship in which he and his wife

had shared a common purpose to provide loving health care to Dr. Wood's patients. Although Mrs. Wood had not had any medical training, I felt certain that the role she chose to play during her lifetime had been a very important one.

I asked, "Do you have any advice for people who are in medicine or business or other professions, who often say that their business comes before their families, even when the wife is not as agreeable as your wife was?"

"I think you should try to strike a happy medium. If you are going to have children, I think you should figure you are going to give time to them. Nothing else is going to make a successful marriage. I do think it is a difficult thing to do if you are in the practice of medicine."

Dr. Wood and his wife had never had children of their own, and I asked him if he had ever regretted it. His answer came as a surprise to me.

"I think from the kid's standpoint, it was better that I didn't have any."

"Because you weren't around that much?" I asked.

"No, I mean whether it would have been the best environment and spirit to grow up in. Fifty years ago, I used to get upset easily, and I had a tendency to get depressed at times, particularly if everything was not going as well as I liked.

"For instance, when I started out it took four or five years before I was reasonably busy, and that was depressing to me. I think that in the last thirty years, I have been interested in what I can do to help other people. I stopped measuring myself, and most people would say I now have a pretty happy disposition. Now I am very easy to get along with. I have changed."

As we spoke, it seemed to me that it might be difficult for a man who had had such a busy medical practice to be in retirement with no schedules to keep and no more responsibilities to his patients. I asked, "How do you spend your time?"

"Oh, I spend it doing plenty of things. I read a good deal. I exercise every morning. I walk two and a half to three miles every morning. I go to medical meetings and listen to lectures. Since retiring I take blood pressures for senior citizens every two months. And I enjoy playing golf a couple of times a week and seeing if I can improve my game. I watch television a fair amount, and I'd say those are my main activities."

In closing our conversation that day, I asked Dr. Wood if there was anything else that he would care to add. I think it was to make sure I had gotten his whole message that he reminded me, once again, "Don't forget to follow the Golden Rule."

Afterword

As I said goodbye and began the drive back to my home, I thought about the many thousands of people whom Dr. Wood and his wife had helped over the more than sixty years they had served their community. They had given both money and time to help make their community and the lives of the people living in it a little better. But they had also given something even more precious, and that was their own care and love. They had truly made this world a better place in which to live, and everything that they had given, from the deepest parts of their beings, continued to flow out into the community.

There was a clarity and simplicity around Dr. Wood that reminded me of the lesson that when we give unconditional love, from the center of our hearts, with no expectations or demands, love goes on forever and never dies.

Through their giving and their caring, Dr. and Mrs. Wood have touched the hearts of thousands of people, setting an example of how each of us, no matter what our job or profession or economic status happens to be, can make a difference. As I thought about these things, Dr. Wood's own words came back to me:

"I had my little contribution to make—and maybe it will help make this world a better place in which to live. My point is, if I can do something that will make this a better place, that is my answer. I think you have to practice, not just preach."

As I think about these words, which have guided Dr. Wood's life, I see them as an inspiration in my own life. Perhaps they can offer the same inspiration to you.

CHAPTER

8

FANNY
RAY

Learn to look on all things
With love, appreciation, and open-mindedness.

In our society today, grandmothers are often the unsung heroes and the angels of mercy. Fanny Ray is a wonderful example of this. She is seventy-one years old and truly is a bright beacon of hope and caring in a place where there is much chaos, lack of hope, and darkness.

As I spoke with Fanny and learned about her work and dedication, I was reminded that so many times we can truly make a difference in the world by focusing our attention on the needs of our own neighborhoods and our own families. Her story is also a reminder that old age is not just a time to rest and be catered to. She teaches that it is always possible to stay in the present, not to allow age or lack of energy to deter us from responding when we hear a call for help or love.

This is the story of just one woman among thousands, demonstrating how grandmothers are truly making a difference. The story is a gentle reminder to all of us that there are many Fanny Rays in our midst, all quietly showing the way to unconditional love, and all more than deserving of our recognition, support, and love.

Fanny, a black woman, lives in the middle of Harlem, in New York City. She was born in New Orleans.

"My mother and father died when I was a teenager," she told me. "I was a model and went into show business. I got out of show business in 1943 when I got married. My husband passed away in 1965. It has not been an easy life, but I have managed."

Fanny Ray is unique but she could just as well be one of the countless numbers of older women the world over. She has taken on the responsibility for raising her grandchildren because her daughter, who is in a drug rehabilitation program, is not available to give the children the love and care they require.

The problems of addiction among single-parent families are becoming greater and greater in our society, especially in neighborhoods where people are living under the extreme pressures of poverty, where it is so easy to feel without hope or faith. At the same time as there has been a significant rise in the number of single-parent families, there has also been an increase in the use of street drugs. Because many single parents were addicts before they were parents, their children are exposed to drugs very early in their lives and sometimes are introduced to them in the womb. While social agencies are expressing much alarm as they so desperately seek solutions to this often ignored problem in our society, it is grandmothers like Fanny Ray who are responding, right now, with their caring and unconditional love for the children.

This is very much a global problem today. I was recently in Central and South America, where there is an alarming increase in the number of children living on the streets. Many of these children were first abandoned by their fathers and then later by their mothers. The numbers of these children would be far greater if grandmothers had not come to the rescue.

When I asked Fanny if she would be willing to share something about her daughter's struggle with drug addiction, she told me, "She has been using drugs for the last ten or fifteen years and I have been taking full responsibility for the children since 1984. When I found out my daughter was really on drugs, I got her involved with Reverend Allen. He has an ARC Drug Program at 1881 Park Avenue. He has a house there where he takes in all kinds of drug addicts. He helps rehabilitate them. They stay there a certain length of time until they get themselves together.

"He makes arrangements for them to go out on jobs. And it is just a wonderful job that he is doing. So my daughter was there, and off and on she would come and go. Now one of the main problems that many of us are having is that when people go off and get addicted to drugs, they forget about their children.

"As soon as I found out my daughter was on drugs, I knew it was up to me to take care of the kids. The kids had a bad life. They were in foster homes, and I didn't like the idea of that. I had to fight to get them back. There is a real money problem. The agency only gives me four hundred dollars per month for all three boys, and with the rent, food, and telephone and light bills, it is very hard to make ends meet. But somehow I manage to do the best I can."

I asked, "Is your daughter still on drugs?"

"No, she hasn't been on drugs for almost a year now. She's still trying to get herself together. She is still on probation, and still involved in different sessions in the rehabilitation program."

It had come to my attention that Fanny's responsibilities were not limited to taking care of her grandchildren. The fact is that her community work has been so extensive that it has attracted the attention of many civic groups. She had recently been given the Woman of the Year award for New York City.

She told me, "I was chosen by the NAACP as the

Woman of the Year in New York because of my work in the community. I am seventy-one years old, and I've got lots of energy except when my heart gives me a bad time. I got the award because they appreciated my work with children and their parents."

I asked her to describe some of the work she did for her community.

"I have been working for the Board of Education for almost twenty-three years," she told me. "I work for the Advocate Resource Center Drug Prevention Program, and I work in School District Three. I am a junior neighborhood school worker. I live in Harlem and there are drug pushers all over the place. There are so many people not just on I.V. drugs but on drugs such as crack. I spend quite a bit of time making visits to the parents' homes. I work with the parents, giving them advice, educating them about drugs, and if the situation is really bad I refer them to agencies and things like that.

"I have helped sick people in my neighborhood and I've talked with many addicts. I'm a community worker. I work in the polls. In the elections I have been an inspector for the last eighteen years.

"I also spend much time being a dance teacher in the district. I teach cultural dancing, and we do shows for the mayor and police department and different programs. The children I work with range from seven to eighteen years of age.

"I've helped a lot of kids. They have to give me a good report card if they are to partake in my dancing. Many young ladies and boys I have had have gone on to college. And I have had some that just dropped out on the way. You know how those things are."

I asked Fanny, "What are some of the most interesting and rewarding experiences you have had doing your work?"

"Helping families. Helping people to come back and realize right from wrong. It has motivated a beautiful friendship with many people and myself, and I have been able to save some lives. For example, I had a mother that walked away from her children and didn't want to be involved with them anymore. I talked to her and showed her another way. I helped get her a job. I have helped a number of people get on welfare."

What Fanny didn't say, but which I knew, was that there were many, many families that had been on the verge of splitting up who she had helped with her own brand of grandmotherly wisdom. She has gotten parents to be more involved with their kids, taking them to places such as the park and the zoo.

I asked Fanny if she would tell me about Harlem and the neighborhood where she lives.

She replied, "Many people are on crack. The neighborhood is infested with it. There are always crack dealers all over the place. They break banisters, and awful things are always happening. But drugs are not just in Harlem. They are everywhere in Manhattan.

"You know," she said, "a lot of children don't get a chance to be with their parents. They don't get the love that they need. I've gotten kids to start going to school regularly. I have helped get clothes for the children because many of them don't have things to wear to school."

"If I brought you into a class of fifth-graders today, and you were going to give them three or four pieces of advice, what would you tell them?" I asked.

"I would tell them that drugs get a person to be a bad person. I would tell them it is just like the boogeyman. You don't play with it. You don't accept it from nobody. I would tell them that people can put drugs into candy. They can give it to you in cookies. I would tell them to always say no to everything that

165

looks bad. Don't get involved with no one that you don't know. I would advise them to be good, to obey their parents, respect their elders, and always be on God's side. Say your prayers at night, learn to love each other, and try not to fight with each other.

"If you can't do anything right, don't do nothing at all. And you must learn to play with each other. You must learn to love one another. And that is what life is all about."

I asked, "Could you tell me about your religious and spiritual background?"

Fanny answered, "I do believe in God. I go to church but I am not there every Sunday. I was Catholic, but I changed over to Baptist because I wanted to be baptized."

"Do you believe that God is helping you in your work?"

"Oh, certainly," Fanny replied. "Where would I be without Him? I know from signs I've had that if it wasn't for my Maker I would not have made it. And I do believe there is a God because I am wonderfully blessed through prayers.

"He has let me live this many years. He has given me my health. I have a little problem with my heart at times, but I don't have no arthritis that holds me back. I go and come. I can still move. I can still do things. In fact, sometimes I don't think I'm seventy-one, but I think I am only fifty-one. I don't look my age and I don't act it."

As our conversation drew to an end, I asked her how she wanted to be remembered after she died. She thought about this for a moment, then replied that she would like to be remembered for: "Helping humanity and for being a helper and a community person for people that are really in need. I want to be remembered for my heart and that I gave my heart to many people trying to help them. I have tried to help the homeless, and I would like them to remember me.

"My daily prayer is for them to have a better world. I want to pray for peace all over the world. And the little while I am here I hope to still help others along the way."

I was very moved by her words. "That is very beautiful," I said. "There are many people, however, who do not feel as you do about helping others and making a difference in the world. Do you have any ideas about why you feel this way, or why so many people don't want to help others or are down on the homeless?"

Fanny answered, "I don't know. I say to myself that my hard times have made happy thoughts. I know that with God's help I am much better off than a lot of people are. I thank God for the courage to continue and for God's love to bless all of the races.

"Let us all be united and have peace. I hope that all wars, corruption, killing, and all this dealing in drugs will disappear. I just hope that I can be one of the people that takes some of the badness out of the world and puts goodness into it and saves humanity from this business that they are heading for."

Afterword

Fanny Ray sums it up most clearly and succinctly: If we are to help humanity and ourselves to make this a better world to live in, we must learn to love one another and help one another. Fanny Ray was not out looking for praise when she felt guided to help children and their families. She was not looking for praise or recognition when she felt guided to take care of her three grandchildren for as long as she was needed. There were no conditions about her love. She truly lives her life from her heart.

I needed to be reminded by Fanny that hard times

can make happy thoughts and that going through our trials and tribulations has the potential of making us stronger and more compassionate people. In my own life, when things are going wrong, there are those days when I feel like a victim and am tempted to become attached to anger. Fanny reminds me that everything that happens to me can be viewed as a positive lesson.

Fanny could certainly have felt that she was a victim in raising her daughter's children, but she saw it as another opportunity to give her love. She seemed to know in her heart that her own healing comes from her willingness to be helpful to others. We teach what we want to learn.

Fanny Ray, and the many others like her, are truly making a difference in this world as they continue to give their limitless love. Fanny refuses to see age as holding her back. And she demonstrates faith and trust that she is not doing it alone.

9

FRANK
MORGAN

I can elect to change
all thoughts that hurt.

On August 9, 1989, I appeared on the nationally tele-
vised *Today Show* with my partner in life, Diane
Cirincione. On the same program was a man by the
name of Frank Morgan, who Bryant Gumble introduced as the top "be-bop" saxophone player in the
world. I was deeply moved hearing the very special
music that came from Frank Morgan's saxophone and
was aware of a peace and light that seemed to shine
from the greatest depths of his soul.

Although I had thought that this book was finished
at the time, after meeting Frank I just knew that I had
to include him. His is the story of a life that was
plagued with repeated failures but that is now ap-
proaching both inner and outer success. And his is the
story of a man who is making a difference in the world
through his music. He teaches us never to give up and
not to be attached to our repeated failures and lack of
success.

I didn't believe that it was an accident or coincidence
that I met Frank when I did—I love the definition of
coincidence as a "miracle in which God wishes to re-
main anonymous." I felt that there was an important
message in Frank's turnaround that I wanted very
much to share with my readers.

After the program we went over to our hotel and met Frank's wife, Rosalinda Kolb, herself a very fine artist. They both consented to an interview for this book. It turned out that Rosalinda had read some of my other books. She told me that *Love Is Letting Go Of Fear* had been the one that really spoke to her. The miracle was that she was just introducing my books to Frank. It was a wonderful meeting, and Frank and Rosalinda were as happy to meet Diane and me as we were to meet them.

When I asked Frank to tell me about his life, I was impressed with his openness and the sincerity of his answers.

"I came from a broken home," he told me. "I felt from early on that neither my mother nor father had much time for me 'though I must say that when I was a baby, my father would play his guitar by my crib whenever he was off the road. They tell me I reached for the instrument right away.

"I was an only child and I was raised by both of my grandmothers. Being a musician, my father was on the road almost all of the time, and my mother wanted to be with him. My father was the leader of the famous Ink Spots, and he is still on the road performing. As a matter of fact at this very moment, at 75 years of age, he is singing with the Ink Spots at the Sheraton Hotel in Waikiki, Hawaii."*

I asked Frank, "At what age did you get interested in music?"

"I think I actually started playing the guitar when I was three or four years old. When I was three I had the opportunity of first hearing the man who many people think was the greatest saxophone player ever to

---

*Shortly after this interview, I received a note from Rosalinda and Frank telling me that Stanley, Frank's father, had passed away.

live, Charlie Parker. When he stood up to play his first solo in that big band, it was like I heard my own voice for the first time. He became my idol and my music teacher, though I also worked hard to be a classical saxophonist.

"The fact that my idol, Charlie Parker, was a drug addict at that time didn't seem like such a big deal. I took it more as a normal way of life, and it seemed normal to identify with that style of life. I think, however, on a deep subconscious level, I later kind of felt that I had to do drugs to understand what my teacher knew. The lesson there was, 'I can't hear what you are saying because what you are doing speaks so loud.' "

I asked, "What about your schooling? What was that like?"

"I was raised in Milwaukee and attended a school that was very similar to the Montessori School. It was a school where you could go at your own pace. I was an excellent student and skipped some grades.

"I came to California when I was fourteen years old. In Milwaukee it was hip to raise your hand in the classroom and to get good grades. I got to California only to find out that it was very 'unhip' to do these very same things. I then went to an all black school where many of the students were street kids.

"I ended up going to Los Angeles City College and began working as a musician. I was nineteen when I first ended up in jail. About a fourth of my life has been spent in and out of jails since that time. I have been into heroin and cocaine in large quantities. I had a big habit for many years, 'though I was never a seller of drugs. I was always just a consumer who did petty crimes—burglary and forgery. I never felt that I could ever really stop taking drugs. And even in jail it was not that hard to get drugs and continue your drug habit."

I then asked Rosalinda to tell me about her perceptions of Frank over the years that she had known him.

"We have known each other about ten years," she replied. "On December 22 we will celebrate our first wedding anniversary. We were married one day before Frank's fifty-fifth birthday. There have been several junctures where I almost gave up on Frank. I remember visiting him in five different correctional institutions over a period of five or six years. There were moments within the span of a number of years when I would stop writing and visiting him.

"Then there were times when I did a lot of visiting and writing and sending him books and gave him a lot of support. Frank is a lovely light, as you said. I have always been able to see that in him, and over the years it has been very frustrating trying to get him to let go of the fear and lean more toward the light in himself. The light has always been there. He is very personable, one of the sweetest people I've ever met. And I want to add that we just celebrated his fourth year of freedom from incarceration."

I turned to Frank and asked, "What happened to make the difference for you, to motivate you to get away from drugs and the life you were leading where you were always ending up in prison?"

Frank replied, "I finally turned it over to God. Rosalinda told me, 'You say you love me and want us to be together. If you really want that, then you have to stop going to prison. You have to play your saxophone and stop abusing yourself.' She said, 'I am not going stand by and watch you kill yourself.' I prayed to God to help me stop going back to prison, to help me work better as an artist, and to give me another chance with Rosalinda and with life. I've gotten everything I prayed for.

"What happened was that I was released from prison

on April 2, 1985, to find that Dick Bock had gotten me a contract for an album with Fantasy Records. That album, *Easy Living*, turned out to be a hit. And then I found myself back on drugs. For the first time ever, I turned myself back in, and I knew somewhere inside of me that this time it was going to be different. I spent four months in Chino and was released on November 8, 1985. This time was going to be the last time. I was not going back on drugs. I went back with a different attitude. It was Rosalinda's love and God's love that made the difference."

I asked, "Do you now think that it's God's work for you to play the saxophone? Is that the way you bring love into the world?"

Frank smiled as he answered, "Yes, I believe that is my assignment. I think that when I do what God gave me the gift to do, to go out into the world and to use that gift with humility, I think the world then unfolds in a harmonious way. There is no other way that I can explain what has happened to me since I got out of prison this last time.

"The July 1989 issue of *Esquire* magazine has a very flattering article about me. There have been articles in *Newsweek*, *People* magazine, *The Atlantic*, many jazz magazines, major newspapers, and CBS's *Sunday Morning* did a feature on me that went nationwide. I want to get my life together now and I particularly want to help kids stay off drugs. I think that you teach by being an example, and my goal is to be an example. I'm tired of lying. It is beautiful to get up in the morning now and say, 'I don't have to lie to anyone today.'

"I can't be that example until I am off my methadone medication or until I have no more desire to smoke pot or do cocaine. Drugs don't really do it for me any more. I don't want to feel guilty and I know the bottom line is that I have to be sober to do what I want to do."

I asked Frank, "What do you feel the most guilty about in your life?"

"I don't really know. I think that maybe it is feeling guilty being black as a kid. Not totally, but something like that."

I then asked, "Who is on the top of your list of people you have not yet totally forgiven?"

"That would be my father. I am working on it, though. I know that right now my father and mother are very proud of what I am doing, and I'm glad that I am doing that while they are still alive."

I then told Frank a little about my own struggle with my addiction to alcohol and what a significant part forgiveness had played in my letting go of the past and letting God into my heart. I told Frank that over and over again I would put off forgiving those who I believed had hurt me even though I knew that holding on to my grievances with them kept me going back to alcohol. When I listened to my ego, I would feel that I was right to hold on to these grievances and never to forgive these people. What had helped me tremendously was to ask myself these two questions each day: "Do I want to be the King of Procrastinators' Club?" and, "Do I want to be happy, or do I want to be right?"

Frank laughed and said, "Those two questions are right on the mark and right up my alley. You know, I can be on stage blowing my horn, and I can feel all the peace and happiness in the world right inside of me, and that is when I feel the presence of God. But once I get off the stage, it isn't all that easy. I have to work at it all the time."

I asked Frank: "After you are gone, how would you like people to remember you?"

"I would like to be remembered as a failure who became a success, who became a successful person, a person who shared his love for the world through his music. I would also like to be an example for others who have given up hope and think they are doomed to failure for the rest of their lives. I would like them to know from my life experience that it is not impossible to stop taking drugs."

Afterword

You cannot be with Frank and Rosalinda without recognizing the light they bring to the world. Although they have been through hell and back they have chosen to have hope and faith in God, in love, and in each other. They have chosen to move beyond the painful experiences of the past and to utilize every experience of their lives as a positive experience for learning.

They are most grateful for the success of their marriage, the success of Frank's musical career, and for the many blessings they are now receiving. Their smiles and the peace they share were contagious and it was an utter delight to spend just a few moments with them.

I found that I could identify very directly with Frank's statement that once he is off stage it is not always easy to stay in touch with the presence of God. Frank reminded me of how quickly the mind can run away from peace, and how necessary it is to discipline our minds each second of the day.

Frank is no longer afraid of failure or success. In his heart he knows that he is an instrument of God, playing the music that goes right to the center of the soul. He has demonstrated for himself, and many others, that there are no limits and that everything is possible when you turn your life over to God.

10

YOU ARE NEVER TOO OLD OR TOO YOUNG TO MAKE A DIFFERENCE

The light has come.

You Are Never Too Old

I heard the story of a man who had worked in middle management all his life and then, long before his retirement, he died suddenly of a heart attack. A short time later his wife and children moved to another city to live with her parents. Many of the people who had worked with this man went to his funeral, and this experience began to raise questions within them. Many of them realized, "This could happen to me!"

One of the things that frightened these people was that not only was this man gone but that after a while it was almost as if he had never been there.

One question that all of this raised was, "When I am dead, how will I be remembered? Has my life been so insignificant that I really didn't make a difference?"

These are not easy questions. Many of us avoid asking them because the answers can be painful. For so many of us the only answers we get feel empty. Perhaps we stop to realize that maybe we will be remembered only because we were a successful salesperson, or that we were always at work on time, or that we got a gold watch when we retired, or that we were a good and fair competitor in sports.

It is my impression that most of us don't give a hoot about being remembered for our punctuality or job performance or how successful we were at earning money. When we are tempted to live our lives as robots, caught up in the routine and humdrum business of the world, or when we spend most of our lives competing to see who is best, or who has the most possessions, we may truly feel that our lives are very empty.

I believe that what really matters to most of us are our heart connections, the love we extend to others from our hearts. This is what really makes our lives matter. Many, many years ago I remember someone saying that living without sharing one's life is a wasted life, and I believe this is true.

As the years pass and we enter that stage of life that some refer to as "old age" or "elderly," there is a temptation to look back on our lives and be disappointed by what we find. And if we look ahead, we see but a few years left, and we may wonder what we have really accomplished. Perhaps we are struck by the feeling that we have had little or no effect on the planet or those who live on it.

How old we are or how many years we have left to live are questions that need not make us feel that our contribution has been small or limited. When it comes to love, there are no big or small gifts. True love is always total and beyond any measurement or comparison.

There are many people who did not learn about giving their total love until rather late in their lives. These are the late bloomers. In my way of looking at it, in God's eyes some flowers bloom early while others bloom late, but all of them blossom and share totally their beauty, magnificence, and love with all who are willing to receive such gifts.

Joseph W. Charles

When I first became aware of Joseph Charles's story, my whole being chuckled and I smiled with delight. I knew that I had discovered a late bloomer who had found his own way to touch the hearts of thousands of people every day of his life. I first saw Mr. Charles on San Francisco's Bay Area television news. A week later I was interviewing him in his home in Berkeley.

The television news had shown Mr. Charles, a seventy-eight-year-old widowed black man, doing what he had done for years. He was standing at the curb in front of his house during the commute hour, wearing white gloves and, like a graceful ballet dancer, waving at all the passengers in the cars going by. And he was wearing a smile as wide as the sky. As the cars went by he would call out to them, "Have a great day! Have a beautiful day! Have a happy day!"

Well, as people learned of this man, they began to drive as much as a half-hour out of their way just to be greeted by him and to start their day with a smile. Here was a man who was making a heart connection with thousands of people every year, and he had begun in his later years.

He told me later, with much pride, that he knows he will be remembered as the man who helped make others feel happy as they started their day. I do believe that the heart memory that people have of Mr. Charles smiling and waving will never fade, and that in his own way he has already made a significant difference.

I was about fifteen minutes early for my appointment with Mr. Charles the day I visited him. I found him still standing at the curb in front of his house, white gloves and all, waving at all the passersby. It so happened that an ABC News team was there from New York, filming him for the evening national news.

I noticed that everyone waved back as enthusiastically and energetically as Mr. Charles waved to them. All kinds of people became involved—families with small children on their way to school, kids on bikes, truckdrivers, commuters, people walking on the sidewalk, smiling and laughing, people honking their horns. And there was Mr. Charles, waving his arms as if in a dance, greeting everyone with "Have a great day! Have a happy day!" When not waving he stood so erect that it seemed as if his head might be touching the clouds, and he looked much younger than his years.

As I watched all this taking place, I remember thinking that there was no way that a person could go by Mr. Charles and still hold on to a "down" or depressed feeling. It was no small wonder that so many people drove miles out of their way so that they could start their day with an "upper" that was filled with love.

Here was a man who was teaching what many of us find so difficult, a man who was starting the day with a smile and with a heart full of love for everyone. Here was a man who was teaching everyone who saw him that it is possible to learn to start each day in a positive way. And it was clear to everyone that all the love and positive feeling he extended to so many was returned a thousandfold. Here was a man who was demonstrating that to give is to receive.

As we went into his modest wood-framed home, I noticed how neat and tidy everything was. There was a lot of fruit and other food in almost every room in the house. Mr. Charles told me he always likes to have extra food available because there are so many needy and hungry people today. He told me that many people just stop by his house for a snack, knowing they will never be refused and that something will always be there for them. He went on to say that there had been a time in his life when he didn't know where his next meal would come from, and now he wanted to give to those who were in need.

I asked Mr. Charles how long he had been known as the waver and how it all began.

"It was on October 6, 1962, and that is over twenty-six years ago. It all started when a neighbor said one day, as I was working in my garden, 'You know that when you wave and smile at me when I go by, it makes me feel so good that I just like to walk by here.'

"He told me, 'I bet there are a lot of other people who could use your help in starting their day with a smile. Why don't you just go out on the street and wave and smile at people going by and help them start their day out right.' "

Mr. Charles paused for a moment, and his eyes looked into the distance as though he was remembering that day. Then he continued, "Well, at first I thought it was a nutty idea and that people would just laugh at me for being a crazy old man. But after a while something spoke from within my heart that simply said, 'Do it!' It was like God talking to me, so one morning I just began."

"What was the initial response?" I asked.

Mr. Charles smiled. "I was amazed at the response. People not only began waving at me, they began to honk their horns, too. I have kept on doing it all these years because I love to speak to people, and with my waving I speak to so many. It seems like they enjoy it, and it makes me feel good because they enjoy it."

And then, with great simplicity and emphasis, he said, "I can make people feel good, and if I can make someone happy I think I am doing something great."

As I was listening to Mr. Charles, I thought of the many times, before I was on a spiritual path, when my heart told me to do something, but, unlike Mr. Charles,

I didn't do it. I didn't do it because I was afraid of what other people might think. And during those days my concern about what other people might think was a top priority.

Mr. Charles was reminding me that when you get a message that comes from your heart, and with love, it is very important to trust it, to go for it. Too many of us go through our lives being limited because we are always concerned about what others might think, living more in our heads than in our hearts.

There is a wonderful organization that was started by some friends of mine. It is called the Giraffes, and it is for those people who are willing to stick their necks out. In my mind, Mr. Charles is a Giraffe because he was willing to stick his neck out and go with his heart, regardless of what people might say.

When I asked Mr. Charles how much time he devotes to his waving, he said, "I am out there five days a week from 7:45 A.M. to 9:30 A.M. I am retired now, but when I first started I was working and I was out there only about forty-five minutes. I was a packer for a naval supply store, packing airplane parts such as wings, rudders, air alarms, and all of that. My wife passed on October 18, 1982, and when this all started she thought I was crazy. She looked out the window the day I started and shouted out to me, 'Joseph, come in the house. You must be crazy to be doing what you are doing.'

"She was really not liking what I did at all until she and I went to Burbank, California, and appeared on *Real People*. Her friends saw her on television and then she became interested in what I was doing."

I asked, "What other national shows have you been on?"

"I have been on *Good Morning America, Evening Magazine*, and *Real People*."

"Mr. Charles," I said, "would you tell me about some of the interesting things that happened to you when you were out there waving?"

He thought for a moment. "Well, I just cannot pick out any one outstanding thing, but I will say that I do remember a couple coming from New York, who lived and worked out here for about six months. They came by and gave me a tie and told me that my waving had made them more cooperative with one another. It had brought them closer together because they would go to work and speak to one another about what I was doing. Then they said that they would laugh and feel good.

"And then there was one time that seven ladies rented a car just to come over and shake my hand. They were from Alabama. That kind of thing makes you feel real good."

"I understand that kids like to come up to you, shake your hand, and get your autograph," I said.

"That is the whole thing in a nutshell," he said. "Those children, I love them. I love everyone, but I really love the children. They come up for my autograph all the time, and that is why I have this stamp with my signature on it."

I noticed he was wearing a cross and I asked him if that meant he was a religious man.

"Well, I will tell you that I am not a churchgoing member or anything like that, but there is a God, and I believe in God. I love the cross. It is beautiful. I don't wear it to be religious. I love it and wear it because I think that it is Christ-like."

With a little encouragement from me, he went on to speak about his beliefs: "I feel Jesus inside of me. It makes me feel good. It gives me a great spirit and releases me from any worries that I may have."

I asked, "Do you feel that Jesus is inside you, telling you what to think, say, and do?"

"That's the truth," he replied.

We then discussed his personal history. He told me, "I only had a fifth-grade education. I had to go to work then because my mother was not able to work and my father had recently died. I had four brothers and two sisters, and I have only one sister left. I was the second oldest and the oldest boy.

"I don't remember much about my dad, but my mom was a beautiful person. She couldn't read or write, but she was always doing unto others as you would wish them to do unto you. That is one of the greatest teachings in the world.

"I never had much education but I do know how to treat people. I treat them just like I want them to treat me. I don't want nobody to hurt me and I am not going to do anything to hurt anyone."

All of us know the Golden Rule, but I rarely meet anyone who puts it into practice with the same commitment as Mr. Charles does. He does not have many years of formal education. But there was one higher "degree" that I felt he demonstrated with every aspect of his being—a degree in Love.

It has occurred to me that many of us who have gone to college and have letters after our names could learn something from Mr. Charles that our formal educations left out. The lesson he teaches is how simple it can be to make a love connection with another person. And what a better world we would live in if we could all take this lesson into our hearts and put it into practice.

Mr. Charles told me about a time when he was robbed and beaten. I asked him how he was feeling about that now, if he was still holding any grievances. His reply: "People are going to be people and that is that. I know in my heart that I forgave him because I don't hold anything in my heart against anybody."

I asked, "If after you die there was to be just one statement on your tombstone, what would you want it to say?"

"I have never thought what I wanted on my tombstone. I don't think I really care. Maybe something like, 'He did his best to do God's work,' like helping people."

I asked, "What advice do you have for people out there who are not smiling?"

"Well, I just say smile and have a good day. That is my advice because you feel good and it looks good if you smile. That is the best I can give anyone. I love to see other people smile."

Somehow we got into discussing politics. (This was just before the 1988 presidential ticket was chosen.) Mr. Charles told me, "I would like to vote for Jackson but I hope he does not win because they are going to kill him if he does. The whites are not ready for blacks right now, not as president, and that is the truth. What he [Jackson] is doing is threatening that they will put a black in there. If he is elected vice president they are going to kill him, too. That is what I think.

"Look what they are doing in these colleges now. The whites against the blacks. You read about it all the time, how they [whites] hate blacks. It is like before the civil-rights movement came on. I don't hate these people but I hate what is happening. I don't hate whites. Some blacks hate whites like I don't know what. I hate that.

"And President Reagan has not been kind to the blacks. He rushes over to Russia, howling about treating people right. Well, they should treat people right right here. President Reagan is smart but I think he is the lousiest president we ever had. He will tell you something and he will turn around and say he did not mean it that way, and they just let him go ahead."

Next I asked Mr. Charles, "What advice might you give to young children who are growing up in the world right now?"

He replied, "Do unto others as you wish them to do unto you. This world has a God. Believe in that God. And get the best education you can."

I asked Mr. Charles to describe to me how he starts each day. He said, "The first thing I do is get down on my knees and pray for about five minutes and thank the good Lord for sparing me. I thank Him for letting me see another day and I thank the Lord for watching over me as I sleep. I thank God for the strength to rise in the morning, to continue to bless me, to continue to put His arms around me as I continue on my daily journey, to bless my family, to bless everyone everywhere."

I asked Mr. Charles what were the most important parts of his life. He replied, "I thank God for having two wonderful sons, which I brought up the best way I could—we got along good. I had a wonderful and beautiful wife. I courted her ten years before I married her and I was married to her for fifty-one years, three months, and thirteen days. I was good at sports and I loved baseball. I love people, and I love that when I am waving, I am meeting new friends all the time, new friends to love, and new friends to be loved by."

As Mr. Charles talked about his prayer of thanks, I was reminded of Meister Eckehart, who once said that the most important prayer in the world is just two words long: "Thank You." If all of us would simply be able to say thank you each moment we are here, no matter what our trials or tribulations, perhaps there would be much more inner as well as outward peace in the world. There was little question that Mr. Charles knew the wisdom in offering his prayers of gratitude.

Mr. Faith

Not too long ago I was in Denver, Colorado, to give a lecture. On the afternoon of the lecture I was asked to see a fourteen-year-old boy who had accidentally been shot by his friend and was completely paralyzed.

It was one of those rare days when I was a bit ahead of schedule and I noticed before leaving for the hospital that there was a shoeshine stand right inside my hotel. Since my shoes needed a shine, I decided to stop. Little did I know what was in store for me. It turned out to be a most remarkable experience and it taught me that there is a master teacher in each of us, even in the person who may be shining your shoes. Although I did not get the name of the man who shined my shoes, I will call him Mr. Faith, for that is surely what he taught me.

First let me tell you of my previous experiences with getting my shoes shined, usually at airports. I would say that although I have never checked it on my watch, the average time it takes to get a shine, from start to finish, is about four minutes, five at the most.

On this day, however, my experience was quite different. Mr. Faith was a black man, about five feet ten, with a smile that went from ear to ear. As he shined my shoes it was as if he was in an altered state of consciousness. He paid no attention to me, totally concentrating on my shoes. He kept stopping, glancing to one side, then the other, and at times it seemed like he was talking to my shoes beneath his breath.

Although I had started reading a newspaper I quickly put it down and became totally absorbed in the man's work. Layer upon layer of new polish was applied to my shoes. And even after they were shining so beautifully that you could almost see your face in them, he continued to polish my shoes.

As I watched Mr. Faith working, he seemed to throw his whole being into shining my shoes. He gave so much care that it was as if he was doing the most important thing in the world. If my shoes had been a person, he could not have been more loving. There were times when he would take his shoe rag and gently go over a small spot, polishing it until it shone brightly. There were other times he seemed to be humming a lullaby or a love song to my shoes.

I began to wonder if maybe my shoes had a special quality that I was not aware of. You see, he seemed almost in a state of ecstasy as he did his work. I have heard Joseph Campbell talk about following your bliss, and although I am not sure I could define what bliss really is I felt this man was clearly following his.

Ten minutes passed, then twenty minutes, and Mr. Faith's enthusiasm continued to be as high as ever. I thought he was treating my shoes as if they were human, as if they were royalty of some sort. Another five minutes went by with no change in the love and tenderness he was giving my shoes. I swear that for reasons I wasn't clever enough to understand, he had absolutely fallen in love with my two-year-old shoes.

I remember thinking that if my shoes could talk they would surely tell me they had never before experienced such unconditional love. I thought to myself that watching this man work was almost like a holy experience, and that at any moment my shoes were surely going to sprout halos and wings and carry me flying out into the street.

After about thirty minutes he finished. It was the first time that he had looked up at me, and if ever I saw the light of love shining with all its glory, it was when I looked into his eyes and saw the joy he had experienced in giving the gift of love not only to my shoes but to me, who happened to be wearing those shoes.

I spoke to him for the first time, saying, "I have to tell you that I have never had an experience like I just had, having my shoes shined with such tenderness, love, and perfection."

My comment seemed to put him at ease, and he replied, "Everything I do is a gift to God. I know that God loves me so much that I know that anything I can do to share his love makes God and me happy. I must be the happiest person on earth because I know it is God's gift to me to allow me to polish shoes with loving care and perfection. I am glad that you like the way your shoes look."

I said, "Like them? I love the way they look! And I admire your total faith and commitment to God." I asked him if he would tell me a little more about his relationship with God.

"Well, I think that life is just a prayer. So I am talking to God all day long, asking for his guidance and blessings and telling him how much I love and appreciate all that He has given me. You see, I know that God is in your shoes and everywhere. God wants me to be tender and gentle and loving to whatever I touch and wherever I am. I normally don't talk about God with people here and I just keep those thoughts to myself. I like to respect my customers' privacy. But you seem to give me permission to talk about God. You know, I sometimes think I have a little ministry right here at my shoe stand."

It was time for me to go to the hospital, and as I left I thought to myself that I had found the light of God being reflected in a shoeshine stand. I also found myself wishing that I had this man's total faith, trust, and commitment to God. There are times when I have felt that way, when I have had experiences of total faith, trust, and commitment to God, but not in the same way as my teacher and new mentor, Mr. Faith.

That night at my lecture, I spent a great deal of time talking about total faith and commitment to love, and I used Mr. Faith as an example. And now on those days when I am having questions about my faith, I think of this man who shined my shoes, and I begin to smile. I remember his total dedication and faith, and it reminds me that I can do that too.

The Clown

As I am getting older—I am now sixty-four—there are days when my body doesn't seem to want to work in the same efficient way it did when I was younger. On those days I am tempted to think that the aging process has its limitations.

Recently, Diane Cirincione and I were having dinner at the home of our dear friends Christine and Wally Amos, in Hawaii. One of their guests was a most delightful seventy-five-year-old woman by the name of Vivian, who taught me a lot that night about not associating limitations with the aging process.

Vivian was full of zest and vitality. When I asked about her age, she answered with a twinkle in her eye that she was "ageless." It became very clear that night that Vivian keeps her heart young by always having a thirst for new experiences and new knowledge.

Vivian told us that she loves to take classes at the local junior college. When I asked her what she was studying at this time in her life, she told me the following story.

Her sister and she went to the college to sign up for an evening course but found that the course they wished to take was filled up. In fact, they were told that every course was filled to capacity except one. When they asked what this course was, they were told that it was a class on how to become a clown.

They laughed and told each other that this would absolutely be the last thing in the world they would be interested in learning. But after further discussion, they looked at each other and said, "Well, as long as we're here, why don't we just go and find out what it's all about?"

They went to the class and were so surprised at how much they loved it that they enrolled that night, and both of them became totally engrossed in the art of becoming a clown. Vivian said how much she enjoyed preparing her "clown self" to bring joy and laughter to others. She said it easily made her forget her own small, insignificant daily problems. She was amazed at what a serious student she became and what hard work it was to learn to be a clown. It took her nearly an hour to create her clown face and put on her costume, and another forty-five minutes to take it off.

Her clown costume is so good that even some of her best friends don't recognize her when she wears it, a fact that Vivian thoroughly enjoys. She says it gives her the freedom to be a totally different person, one who isn't afraid to do and say things that she never knew she was capable of doing and saying.

After graduating from the clown class, Vivian and her sister decided they wanted to be with children and to make them laugh, but they also wanted to spend time bringing more joy and laughter to older people. As a result of their unique spirits, they have become quite well known in their home state of Illinois, and many newspaper and magazine articles have been written about them.

We were absolutely absorbed with Vivian's story, so she agreed to meet with us again the next day. She shared some articles and photos of her and her sister dressed as clowns. And do you know what? No one could ever have guessd their ages. They were indeed ageless, just as Vivian had said the night before!

Vivian stated that becoming a clown is one of the most wonderful things that could ever have happened to her. It gives her a way to give back in gratitude all the love she has received in her life. She feels so good about herself because she feels useful. It is her unique way of making a difference in people's lives. She knows that each day she brings joy and happiness to people of all ages.

Vivian awakens in me, and I think in almost everyone else she meets, the happy, innocent child that each of us has in the center of our hearts. She made it very clear that she lives only in the present and does not worry about the past or the future.

Vivian seems to have known, from the very depth of her being, that the way to heal yourself of irritation, sadness, or unhappiness is to do your best to reach out and help others. She is a true messenger of love, of happiness and humor. She vividly demonstrates that when you don't believe there are any limitations or barriers to expressing your potential and being useful, then there truly are none.

You Are Never Too Young

Our society often teaches us that wisdom comes only with age. Another way of looking at the world is to believe that our true perceptions of wisdom have little to do with how old we are, but much to do with how willing we are to see every person we meet, regardless of their age, as a teacher of love. This means that a three-year-old has as much to teach us as a ninety-three-year-old. I know that my whole life has changed since I have accepted this premise.

I think that it is extremely important to take a whole new look at what we tell our children. For example, children so often hear us say that you can't do this or you can't do that until you are older and are a grown-up. Some children get the erroneous message that they can't be fully alive and make a difference in this world until they are adults. Nothing could be further from the truth.

I have been very fortunate to have worked most of my life with children, and I can attest to what a difference they can make in this world and to what powerful teachers they have been for me. We have so much to learn from them about keeping our imaginations open, with no limits, and to helping create a world without war, a world without obstacles or limitations, a world where there is only love and peace. You are never too young to make a difference, and the following stories are examples of young people who have made significant contributions in their lives.

Some years ago, a boy who we'll call Bill, who lived in a small town in Florida, heard that the Russians were our enemies. He began to wonder about the Russian children and could not believe that they could be his enemies, too. He decided to do something about it. He wrote a short note:

> Dear Comrade in Russia,
> I am writing to a six-year-old friend in Russia. I am seven years old and I believe that we can live in peace. I want to be your friend, not your enemy.
> Will you become my friend and write to me?
> Love and Peace,
> Bill

He then folded his note, put it neatly into an empty bottle, and threw it into the water. Well, the water happened to be an inland lake, and about five days later someone found the bottle with the note in it about thirty yards from where Billy had stood on the beach and thrown it in.

A story about Billy's note appeared in the local newspaper, then the Associated Press picked it up, and pretty soon the story was being published all around the world. A group of people from New Hampshire who were taking children to the Soviet Union as ambassadors of peace read the article. They contacted this boy and his family and invited them to come to the Soviet Union with them. So the little boy, accompanied by his father, ended up going to the Soviet Union a few weeks later. And what a wonderful peacemaker he was!

I love the innocence and simplicity of this story. This little boy had very little past experience to interfere with his thoughts about what might be possible. He decided that he could make a difference and he acted on that. He didn't see any difficulties ahead, nor was he even aware that by throwing the bottle into a lake, rather than the ocean, it would never reach Russia. He somehow trusted that miracles could happen, and they did. In fact, he did much better than he ever dreamed, eventually delivering his message to the Soviet Union in person. For me this story demonstrates that when you come from the purity of love in your heart, nothing is impossible. It also gives life to the biblical saying that "a little child shall lead them."

There are other stories about children who have led the way. The one that comes to my mind at this moment is the unforgettable story of Samantha Smith. Samantha lived in Maine, and when she was ten she wrote a letter to Yurei Andropov, then the Soviet premier, sharing her concern about the tensions between our two countries. Here is what her letter (dated December 1982) said:

Dear Mr. Andropov,

My name is Samantha Smith. I am ten years old. Congratulations on your new job. I have been worrying about Russia and the United States getting into nuclear war. Are you going to vote to have a war or not? If you aren't, please tell me how you are going to help to not have a war. This question you do not have to answer, but I would like to know why you want to conquer the world or at least our country. God made the world for us to live together in peace and not to fight.

Sincerely,
Samantha Smith

Several months later Samantha received a note inviting her and her parents to visit the Soviet Union. After visiting in Moscow in July 1983, she flew to Simferopol, in the Crimea, where she met with the Pioneers, a Russian youth group. She then went on a boat trip through the Black Sea and flew on to Leningrad. After that they returned to Moscow.

At the time this happened there was great tension and distrust between our countries, with no signs that things might get any better. Samantha became a "peace ambassador" and immediately captured the hearts of children and adults wherever she went. There was a special light and energy that seemed to radiate from Samantha, and she seemed to touch the hearts of everyone she met.

There were pictures and articles about her in all of the Russian newspapers and magazines. She was often seen on Soviet television. She became a celebrity overnight as it seemed that all of Russia was taking her into their hearts. This little ten-year-old girl gave hope not only to the people of the Soviet Union but to millions of people back in the United States.

Samantha's innocence, simplicity, and honesty were almost magical, endearing her to everyone she met. In every sense of the word, she was truly a peace ambassador, who was convinced that there is another way of living in this world other than going to war and fighting each other.

The Russians named a flower after her. They also issued a postage stamp with her picture on it. Pictures and statues of Samantha began appearing in many public places. She became a symbol of new hope for peace and friendship. She wrote a book, *Journey to the Soviet Union*, and was on many television shows, including Johnny Carson's. She began a pilot television series with Robert Wagner.

Throughout the Soviet Union there was not a child or an adult who did not recognize Samantha's picture and know her name. This also became true in the United States. Everyone admired her and saw her as a teacher of peace. She probably did more than any other single person at that time to act as a catalyst for creating harmony, peace, and friendship between our countries.

Then, on August 25, 1985, there was a terrible tragedy. Samantha and her father were killed in an airplane crash. Her untimely death shocked the world. To this day her name continues to be a household word in the Soviet Union, and she is a hero to the many thousands of people, of all ages, who know of her. Her mother has established the Samantha Smith Center in Hallowell, Maine. The main project of the center is its Youth Exchange, with Soviet and American kids attending camps in each other's countries.

A diamond, an asteroid, and a star have been named after Samantha. The state of Maine has established a

Samantha Smith Day, to be celebrated the first Monday of every June. Samantha Smith will always be remembered as the child who opened the door to thousands and thousands of other children visiting back and forth between our two countries, serving as peace ambassadors.

Today, things are quite different between our countries than they were back in 1983. Tensions and distrust are greatly reduced and there is much more hope among the people of both countries. I believe, as do so many others, that Samantha played a most important part in helping to change attitudes in both countries.

In 1981 I started the organization called Children as Teachers of Peace, to bring together children from different countries and to encourage them to express not only their fears about war but their hopes for peace. The children created a book based on what peace meant to them. They told what they would say if they were consultants to a world leader about peace and the leader would really listen.

In 1982, Pat Montandon began to support Children as Teachers of Peace and, like so many others, initiated projects of her own. Later that year, she took a small group of American children, the first such group of its kind, into the Soviet Union, and subsequently to many other nations, to meet with world leaders on the subject of peace. Pat later formed her own organization called Children as the Peacemakers.

In 1986, Diane Cirincione and I, who are co-directors of Children as Teachers of Peace, took forty-eight children between the ages of seven and seventeen, from all over the United States, to the Soviet Union. On the plane coming back, an eleven-year-old boy told me, "I think there are going to be thousands and thousands of kids going back and forth between the Soviet Union and the United States. There are going to be so many friendships that when we grow up, no one will want to hurt anyone or ever go to war again."

And as he was telling me this, I was thinking of Samantha and feeling her light shine brighter than ever through this boy, giving hope to all. Once again I found myself thinking about the biblical saying that "a little child shall lead them," and I knew how true this really is.

World peace is not the only area of concern where children are making a difference. In Philadelphia, an eleven-year-old boy by the name of Trevor Ferrell was watching television one night when he saw a story on the news about street people. His heart ached when he saw these people sleeping in the streets on that bitterly cold night. Although it was late, he told his parents that he wanted to go to these people that night and help them. He just knew that there must be something he and his parents could do to help.

His father was pleased that his son was sensitive to the street people's suffering and that he wanted to help, but it was very late and everyone in the house was tired. Trevor, however, still wanted to go. He was not going to believe in any kind of limitation in following what his heart was directing him to do.

Trevor did not let up. Finally his parents agreed to take him to the center of Philadelphia where the television program had shown the street people to be living. Trevor took a single yellow blanket and a pillow from his own bed. While they were driving, he pressed the blanket and pillow against the car heater to warm them.

As they turned a corner in the city, Trevor saw a man sleeping in the street on an iron grating. He called out to his father to stop the car. Then he calmly got out, walked up to the man, knelt down beside him, and handed him the blanket.

"Here, sir," he told the man. "Here's a blanket for you." Then Trevor went back to the car and brought the man the pillow. The man's face lit up with one of the biggest smiles Trevor had ever seen.

"Thank you," the man said. "God bless you."

"God bless you," Trevor said.

Trevor and his parents were deeply moved by this experience. The next night and the next they returned, bringing blankets and hot coffee for the street people.

But even this was not enough for Trevor. He kept telling his parents, "There must be something more that we can do." There seemed to be no way that this boy was going to give up his idea of helping the street people. He did not sit down and draw up a logical plan but he did follow his heart.

Trevor began putting posters up all over town, asking for donations to help the street people. The response could not have been more heartwarming. People from everywhere brought warm clothes and blankets and piled them high in Trevor's garage to be taken to the street people. One person even donated a Volkswagen van so that they could take the donations to the people who so desperately needed them.

Over time, Trevor's Campaign, as it was named, was helping to feed and clothe and even provide housing for the homeless people in the inner city. There just seemed to be no stopping the enthusiasm and generosity that people from the community showed once Trevor got it started. A whole change of consciousness began to occur. Everyone began to feel better about themselves. Schoolchildren, businesspeople, even people from high society showed up to volunteer their time.

Even the most complacent and doubtful people began to learn that they too could make a difference. People of all ages turned up to help, not only by giving money but by touching the hearts of the people around them who needed their assistance.

One day Trevor's father found a handwritten letter that had been left in the van they used to take food and clothing to the street people. The letter told the story of how this person had lost everything he had ever valued in his life and was now living in the streets. All hope seemed to be gone for him. The rest of the letter, published in *Trevor's Place*, by Frank and Janet Ferrell (published by Harper & Row, New York, 1985) told how all this had changed. The letter said:

> Suddenly, there in front of me stood a little boy with a face of Spring, who gave me a respectful, "Here, sir, I have a blanket for you." He had given me more than a blanket, he gave me new hope. I could not keep back the tears. I fell in love with that little boy named Trevor and at the same time I fell in love again with life.

In 1987 Diane Cirincione and I traveled with some children to Central America, where they visited with other children. In some of the countries we visited, the children had an opportunity to share their thoughts and feelings about peace with the presidents of those countries. While there the children were shown on national television, back in the United States.

One of the children with us was an eleven-year-old boy by the name of Nathaniel Girard. Nathaniel wore dark, Hollywood-style glasses that he rarely took off. To say he was "attached" to them would be an understatement. He was definitely the "Mr. Cool" of our group. We spent three days in Nicaragua and during this time our kids were paired off with children from Nicaragua. The bonding and the friendships formed were immediate and powerful.

We visited many homes, schools, and orphanages, and I don't think that our children had ever seen such poverty before. Our children and their new friends went to the airport together when it was time for us to fly on to Costa Rica. As the children said their good-byes, there were many tears. And then we noticed that Nathaniel had taken off his dark glasses. We stood there amazed and delighted as he handed the glasses to his new friend to keep.

Can there be anything more giving than giving the thing that you prize the most in your life? Watching Nathaniel that day in the airport as he handed over his dark glasses to his friend was such a tender moment. I thought to myself, *This is what unconditional love is all about. It is when you are willing to give your all to another person, asking nothing in return.* For that moment, Nathaniel was not thinking about himself. He had put all his energy into giving his total love to his friend. All his previous self-absorption and self-centeredness had vanished.

A few days after we got home, we received a telephone call from Nathaniel's mother. She said that Nathaniel came up to her and said, "I've just thrown all my G.I. Joe war toys into the garbage can. From now on I am going to devote my life to working for peace." Soon after this, Nathaniel began speaking to groups. He spoke at an assembly for his school, and he spoke at a board of education meeting. In about four weeks he had made ten talks and had also appeared on local radio and television programs.

Later that year, Diane and I returned to Nicaragua and Nathaniel found out that we were going back to visit the orphanage that he had visited. He called us on the phone and told us that he had been saving his money and he was sending us twenty-two dollars to give to the orphanage.

Nathaniel is making a difference. He has had an experience of the heart and I don't think he will ever forget it. He has empowered himself to know that he has an important part to play in this world, and he has made a decision to make peace his number-one priority. He now knows that you don't have to be an adult to make a difference.

I think that we all, myself included, have much to learn from Nathaniel. It is high time for all of us to begin to listen to the voices of children.

For a number of years I have had the dream that one of the ways that our world could be transformed from fear and hatred to love and peace would be to have children, as a regular part of their school curriculum, be involved in volunteer programs where they are helping others. When love and caring are put into action by our educational system, many wonderful things can happen.

For the past two years, children from kindergarten up to the eighth grade have been involved in just such a project at the Waldorf School in Santa Cruz, California. This special program is called Willing Hands, Caring Hearts. Each class in the school has its own program. One class might adopt a nursing home, another might choose to be with families who have physical disabilities, while another might choose to work in a soup kitchen, helping to feed the homeless.

This year the kindergarten class raised their own vegetables and took them to a local soup kitchen, then helped to prepare meals. Then, they sat down at the tables and ate with the homeless. All these are ongoing progams, so friendships are formed and relationships develop between people.

The children who have been working with the aged, going into retirement, nursing-care homes, and senior centers have had particularly rich experiences. Because it is an ongoing program, the children get to know the names of the people they help. They keep records of when they were born and they send them birthday cards on their birthdays. Sometimes the children run errands for the elderly. They paint fences and do gardening for those who still have private homes. Perhaps more important than all the many practical things they do are the hugs and love that they give and receive. They are truly learning that to give is to receive.

In many cases, the children who work with the elderly have had the opportunity to grow very close to people who later died. Their experiences in this have been particularly rewarding, though at first many people who hear about it think it must be very sad as well. It has allowed the children to learn about their feelings concerning life and death that they simply could never have known if they'd been isolated in their classrooms.

The author Hugh Prather, who is a dear friend of mine, has two sons in this program, and one day I asked him to share his impressions of his children's experiences with me. He said, "I believe that this program bridges the gap between youth and old age that has developed in the last several decades in our country. It is most important for young children to get to know elderly people, and this program provides that. The children experience unselfish giving and the reality of oneness of all life, regardless of age and economic conditions."

In addition to bridging the gaps between the elderly and the very young, these programs have also helped to bridge socioeconomic gaps. Last year the children of this school were brought together with children from low economic backgrounds, mainly Mexican-American immigrant children, through an all-day program of doing crafts together and playing baseball and other games.

The people of Santa Cruz have welcomed these projects, and Willing Hands, Caring Hearts has done much to stimulate a new awareness of helping, caring, and loving throughout the community. There is no question in my mind that the children who are taking part in these programs are truly making a difference. I am convinced that by becoming involved with other people in these ways, these children will grow up to be adults who make caring for and helping others a priority in their lives. Already the Willing Hands, Caring Hearts program at the Waldorf school has inspired other schools, both public and private, to get similar projects started for their students.

We have so much to learn from children. And as we join them in giving, the world we live in can become a better place, filled with more light and love than perhaps any of us can imagine.

I find it fascinating that children are not interested in the endless logical or rational explanations for why something can or can't be done. Children have so much to teach us about heart connections—that is, about living in our hearts rather than in our heads.

One of the many wonderful things children teach us is that the problems we perceive as complicated or impossible often have answers and solutions that are not complicated at all. They remind us that love is the answer to all of our problems. They remind us that only through our own helping hands and caring hearts can we create a loving and peaceful world.

Afterword

The adults and children in this chapter make it very clear that age does not have to be a limiting factor in making a difference. When you truly believe that nothing is impossible, then indeed nothing is impossible. Unfortunately many of us, as we reach the later years, spend much of our time reliving the past or absorbed in fears about the future.

As I continue to learn more about seeing everyone as my teacher, regardless of their age, I am finding all kinds of new possibilities and creative ways of living in this world. At one time in my life I had some fears about getting older and I had fears about limitations that I might experience. Now I not only believe but I know that there will always be an unlimited source of creative love energy in my heart, just waiting to be tapped. I do believe that the secret of tapping that fire of compassionate love is continuously to ask the question, throughout every second of the day, "How can I be more helpful and more loving to others?"

I remember a fourteen-year-old boy named Will, who was close to death, giving advice to other kids with cancer. He said, "As long as we are breathing, no matter what is happening to our bodies, our main job is to give our love to others."

One of the many wonderful things that children teach us is that solutions to what we perceive as problems need not have complicated answers. They remind us that Love is the answer to all of our problems. They remind us that helping hands, caring hearts, and the compassion to want to be truly helpful to others can do much to bring about a more loving and peaceful world.

How We Can All Make a Difference Today

Within each of our hearts is an endless list of creative things that we can do to make a difference. This list is revealed to us simply by asking ourselves each day how we might be helpful to others and what we might do to bring more light and love to our planet.

It is possible to start each day letting these two thoughts fill our hearts with compassion and determination, as if our very lives depended on it. I am really talking about a commitment to save our lives and our planet—being very clear that our purpose every day is to help and love others and the vast Universe of which we are all a part.

This means being totally committed to going through each day having the same concerns and interests for others as we have for ourselves. It means focusing our concern beyond our own selfish interests.

Not long ago I heard Roger Muller, formerly of the United Nations, suggest that we can all start becoming global citizens and peacemakers by simply closing our eyes and visualizing the kind of world we'd like to have.

So here is the beginning of a list of questions we can ask, and things we can do, right now, to make a difference:

1. I shall ask each day, what can I do to be more helpful to other people?
2. I shall ask each day, what can I do to bring more light and love to this planet of ours?
3. I will visualize in my mind an image of the kind of world I'd like to live in.
4. I will be reminded that my thoughts as well as my actions help determine the kind of world I live in. Thus I shall ask for help each day to let go of all my attack thoughts and actions—and have them replaced with only loving thoughts and actions.
5. I shall ask what I might do each day to help our handicapped, our elderly, our sick, and our children.
6. I will read and do at least one of the things recommended in the book *Fifty Things You Can Do to Save the Earth*, published by The Earthwork Group, Berkeley, California.
7. I will ask myself what I might do this day in my family, my school, my place of work and during

my leisure hours to make the world a better place to live.

8. There is a wonderful organization called "The Giraffe" for people who are willing to *stick out their necks* to help make the world a better place to live. I, too, will ask myself how I might stick out my neck to make a difference.

9. I will either make a phone call or tell someone in person how much I love them.

10. I will think of someone I have not forgiven and will have a willingness to forgive them today.

This instant is the only time there is.

The time has come to let go of fear because fear is the cause of apathy and indifference to the suffering in this world. The time has come to awaken to the truth that our own suffering begins to dissolve the moment we reach out our hand to be helpful to another soul.

The time has come for each of us to have faith and to trust in love. The time has come to stop being afraid of love and to see the light of love, and nothing else, in each other and ourselves. We heal ourselves, our relationships, and the planet when we become aware that each of us truly does make a significant difference when we make it our top priority to live each moment finding more creative ways for being a little kinder, a little more tender, gentle, helpful, and loving to each other and to ourselves.